HYGGE & LAGOM

A Complete Guide to Change Your Habits,
Declutter Your Life and Create a Cozy Living Space.
Learn the Scandinavian Ways of Living a Balanced
Life Filled with Mindfulness and Happiness

By Linda Meik

regardless of the end form the information ultimately takes. This includes copied versions of the work both physical, digital, and audio unless express consent of the Publisher is provided beforehand. Any additional rights reserved.

Furthermore, the information that can be found within the pages described forthwith shall be considered both accurate and truthful when it comes to the recounting of facts.

As such, any use, correct or incorrect, of the provided information will render the Publisher free of responsibility as to the actions taken outside of their direct purview. Regardless, there are zero scenarios where the original author or the Publisher can be deemed liable in any fashion for any damages or hardships that may result from any of the information discussed herein. Additionally, the information in the following pages is intended only for informational purposes and should thus be thought of as universal. As befitting its nature, it is presented without assurance regarding its prolonged validity or interim quality. Trademarks that are mentioned are done without written consent and can in no way be considered an endorsement from the trademark holder.

Table of Contents

Part I: Hygge

CHAPTER 6: HOW TO MAKE HYGGE PART OF YOUR LIFE

Part II: Lagom

PART I: HYGGE

Introduction

For some reason, we cannot seem to keep life simple and happy. Perhaps, it is because of too many wants. It could be the need to make money, and when we see something we desire we want more of it. When we are not making enough money we tend to become stressed, desire even more material things, and life suddenly becomes unhappy.

Statistics show an increase in ill-health due to stress. Doctors and psychologists are agreeing that stress needs to be managed. There are not enough people who seek help for their stress or if they do, they are not getting enough help. Somehow many of us get stuck in a rut, where we no longer take care of ourselves.

Despite the conveniences of modern life, too many people suffer from constant stress, anxiety, and depression. Experts will tell you that part of the problem is that most people are looking for happiness in all the wrong places. Some see happiness as something abstract in their future, once they have achieved the goals that they set for themselves. Others attach happiness to buying the newest gadgets, staying abreast of the latest trends, and doing what the Joneses do; but anyone who equates happiness to tangible possessions is surely setting themselves up for failure.

The common denominator that these pursuits have is to not be fulfilled with the world around you. It tells you that the present moment is not good enough and you need to do more to make it better. But the truth is that it's a much simpler endeavor to be happy and content with what you have; live a simple life, cut out the distractions, and invest more in people and experiences than possessions to add real meaning to life.

In our modern-day world, one nation that seems to have nailed this ethos is Denmark. The Danish people have long lived by a concept known as Hygge that makes them one of the happiest people on earth. This is a philosophy that reflects the values of the Danish society of equality and wellbeing for everyone. At its core, this is a sense of contentment that removes stress-causing elements in life.

This makes them successful at making the best of what they have and appreciating the small things in life. Since the outdoors is bleak, they create bliss in being indoors. Since the outside world remains dark for long hours, they light up the indoors. And since staying outdoors is uncomfortable overall, they up the coziness factor indoors.

The key here is to be happy and find meaning in things and experiences that make you happy. Life needs moments of pleasure, and the more the better. Pleasure brings happiness and ultimately contentment. Hygge facilitates all this.

It could also be a candlelit dinner with friends. Or, if you wish to take it outdoors, Hygge could be a picnic beside the riverside during the day or roasting marshmallows on a campfire at night.

The crux of living a Hygge lifestyle is that there is no price point to it. It is accessible to anyone who finds anything satisfying, stress-free and comforting. It is an experience meant to be felt rather than something that is created.

Another aspect to Hygge, that many people miss entirely caught up in their hectic lives, is to slow down and savor the present. In overstretched, intricate lives, Hygge uncomplicates the complicated and keeps you affixed to your surroundings. You learn to extract pleasure from what you have around you and not from what you might have one day. This makes living in the present the essence of Hygge.

While considered a Danish concept by origin, Hygge is by no means restricted to the Danish lifestyle alone. It is a lifestyle for everyone because so many of its fundamentals can easily be incorporated into daily life everywhere.

But if you need a little help in how to bring the Hygge factor into your life and home, this book will let you do just that regardless of where you reside. It will familiarize you with Hygge principles and how this lifestyle can let you better take care of yourself and your loved ones.

Chapter 1: What is Hygge?

The word Hygge is hard to pronounce and just as hard to pin down the precise meaning of. The closest translation for it in English would be 'coziness', but Hygge involves much more than just being cozy.

Regardless of the time of year, it's all about community, engaging with those around you, enjoying the simplicity of everyday conversation, laughter and all those other little pleasures in life.

In essence, Hygge refers to a concept that is deeply rooted in Danish and Norwegian culture. As it is a cultural norm in Scandinavia, it might explain why people in this area experience a higher quality of living than other cultures. Hygge is linguistically versatile and can be used to refer to all aspects of life in the form of a noun, verb, or adjective.

As far as its practical implications, Hygge is extremely useful for self-care as well as tending to both the mind and body in the cold winter months. Many scholars believe that is how the concept began: It made the winter more bearable and comfortable for the early Scandinavians.

Specifically, Hygge can work for individuals, couples, families, and anyone who wants to feel better and more mindful of their experiences. Another way to determine whether or not Hygge is right for you is to consider what makes someone more receptive to living the Hygge way.

To contemplate if the Hygge lifestyle is right for you, try asking yourself these key questions:

- **Am I stressed out by everyday life?** There are many ways to deal with the stress of daily life. For many who give it a try, Hygge can help reduce the overall sense of stress and emotional and psychological trouble. Practicing a Hygge lifestyle helps you slow down and take everything one step at a time. It also helps you live in the moment and enjoy the time you spend doing the things you love, so you feel more capable of dealing with the things you may not like so much.

- **Do I feel like I need to recharge my mind?** Hygge can be a great way to recharge mentally. Keep in mind that Hygge is about staying in the present and practicing mindfulness as much as possible. For this reason, keeping Hygge in your heart can enable your mind to feel more rested and recharged more often, too. If you feel overwhelmed all the time by the events and people around you, be sure to take some time for mindfulness as well as self-care. These proactive measures can make a big difference in improving your feelings daily. They also increase your emotional and mental resilience.

- **Do I have trouble coping with changes or problems?** Both can be scary, and while some people can address these situations with dignity and ease, others may lack coping mechanisms, causing stress and panic. If you're someone who isn't sure how to deal with uncertainty or pressure, Hygge can assist you. By remaining mindful and taking care of yourself and your feelings, you can use Hygge to feel better about problems that may arise. Although you may not be able to completely solve every issue with Hygge, it's a great tool to help you feel calmer in the face of adversity.

- **Am I always thinking about money, work, or some other stressful part of my life?** Bring Hygge into your finances, your job, your romantic relationship, your family, and any other part of your life that may be causing you to feel overwhelmed. The more you focus on a source of stress—like work, for example— the more it consumes you and keeps you from living your best life. When you allow Hygge to influence your life instead, you will be able to work through these kinds of daunting issues more effectively. Hygge can allow you to feel comfortable and safe even when you're dealing with dilemmas and chaos in other aspects of your life.

- **Do I want less clutter?** If so, Hygge may be a perfect solution for you. This lifestyle is all about reducing clutter and keeping things as minimal as possible. Although you do not have to give up everything for Hygge, you should be willing and able to abandon a little bit here and there to make your life less cluttered and confusing overall. You'll use minimalistic furnishings and items in your home when you live the Hygge way, and you won't keep a bunch of unnecessary junk. The more you work on downsizing, the more organized your home and life will become. Engaging in this practice can help you feel calm and more Hygge than ever before!

- **Do I feel like I never have a chance to take care of myself?** Self-care is a big part of Hygge, so if you're worried about not being able to take care of your own feelings and needs, this lifestyle may work well for you. However, it's important to remember that Hygge is not about putting yourself first. Instead, it is about making equal time for yourself and for everyone important in your life, too. Don't neglect your friends and family in favor of your needs, but don't abandon your needs either. Finding the right balance will help you feel at ease and will improve your Hygge experience.

- **Do I value things that are comfortable and cozy?** If you love to be physically comfortable and surrounded by things with soft, pleasant textures, Hygge is the lifestyle for you. Hygge is about making sure you have both sensory and aesthetic comfort available to you at all times. To illustrate, decorating with soft, comfortable fabrics and gentle lines and textures throughout your home is a major part of Hygge– though it's important not to overdo the décor, or spend too much money on it, either. Keep things simple and easy when you decorate, and you'll be able to enjoy that comfort even more in no time.

- **Would it be nice to have more time for the things and people I care about?** Sometimes, it may feel like you can't make enough time for your friends, your romantic partner, your colleagues, or your kids. No matter what you try to do, does it seem like someone is always excluded from your plans? If you feel this way frequently, you may need to try regrouping with Hygge. Hygge can help you organize your time better and make sure everyone you care about is getting an equal share of your energy and time. You can also spend time being comfortable and cozy with the people you care about to improve your Hygge experience as well.

these questions only start to explore the reasons why you may be interested in Hygge. Just keep them in mind while you're trying to figure out whether or not this lifestyle is conducive for you. Hygge is very forgiving, so if you try it and find that it doesn't work for you, there's no reason to feel discouraged or guilty. This attempt just means you haven't found the right lifestyle plan yet, and that's okay!

WHY COZINESS?

What is it about being cozy that makes it such a valuable feeling, and such an integral part of Hygge? Coziness helps you feel comfortable and safe. This feeling encourages you to slow down, to consider your experiences and surroundings, and to take time for yourself while also giving your time to others. When you're cozy, you're more likely to be happy, content, and at peace with yourself and the world around you. Practicing Hygge will help you increase your coziness in no time.

But is it that easy to be cozy? Is it beneficial to try practicing such a lifestyle when the world around you is so hectic? Many people believe trying to be cozy and comfortable in all aspects of life is futile. Critics feel that taking too much time to relax will prevent individuals from being ready to face problems and situations that might arise in their day to day lives. These critics insist that Hygge practitioners will be unprepared for the twists and turns of life if they're too busy taking care of themselves to pay attention to the stressful world around them.

However, practicing Hygge and coziness does not imply that you're unprepared or not paying attention to the world around you. being cozy and relaxed can help you better face problems when they do arise. In essence, Hygge can help make it easier for you to cope when things go badly. The more comfortable you are during the good times, the more rested your brain will be when it needs to address problems. You'll also be able to heal emotionally from life's inevitable stresses when you practice a cozy lifestyle, too.

There are many reasons why you might want to incorporate coziness into your life. There's more to it than just being comfortable, and you may be able to find new ways to face life in all its forms when you make Hygge a key part of your regular lifestyle.

THE DON'TS OF HYGGE

Certain things will not fit the Hygge lifestyle. This section will help you understand what is and is not Hygge beyond what has already been discussed.

- Do not force the Hygge lifestyle on yourself or others. It is okay if you want to find a cozy, simple space to live in, but not everyone is ready to leave behind their busy life and join in.

- Do not kick someone out of your social gathering because they cannot keep to the rules. Instead, ask if they would like to be a part of a different social gathering that does not enforce the Hygge lifestyle.

- Do not think you have to be at home or in a social gathering to be Hygge. You can be pleasant to everyone, never being controversial or negative at all times. You can also enjoy a little relaxation to unwind and get rid of your stress even at work.

Take a moment to look at a picture frame you made or something your child made for you. Have a comfortable sweater or take off your shoes to enjoy the carpet in your office, as a way to feel a little Hygge even with all the business going on around you.

RULES OF HYGGE

There are rules to the Hygge lifestyle. You may ask why. If the lifestyle is supposed to be simple and cozy, why does it need rules? Why would you want to follow something that has rules? Is it a religion because it has rules? It is not a religion and you do not have to follow the rules at every turn. When you are having a Hygge moment, then you should make sure you know the rules and do not break them. The rules are to ensure you can be comfortable and get the most benefit out of Hygge. To truly become happy, you need to adopt what makes the lifestyle work. These rules have been given different definitions by experts, so even those who teach Hygge do not always agree on the exact rules.

One website says there are only five rules instead of ten.

1. Establish a comfortable atmosphere
2. Be present in the moment

3. Take pleasure from cozy, simple living

4. Treat everyone as equals

5. Show gratitude, never negative emotions

6. Be comfortable and provide comfort

7. Gather in harmony

8. Be true to yourself

9. Enjoy togetherness

10. Have a shelter

The rules should seem fairly easy to follow. You are asked to treat anyone who comes to a Hygge party with equality, harmony, and fairness. You are meant to have a cozy, comfortable atmosphere, with comfortable seating, where you can enjoy your shelter, whether you have a gathering or remain alone in your shelter.

Chapter 2: Origin of Hygge

Interestingly, the origin of the word Hygge is not Danish but Norwegian and old Nordic. It came into the Danish language in the 18th century but may have only started gaining momentum in the 19th century when the Danish empire crumbled at that time and lost its grandeur to Germany, Sweden, Iceland, and Norway.

Thereafter, the Danes started to identify with simplicity where the military loss was not viewed as a defeat but considered a gain. Instead of focusing on a lack of something, Danes take what they have and create the best of it. As such, many believe that the term could resonate with Danes because of their country's history.

The Denmark that emerged was heavily influenced by the teachings of Nikolaj Frederik Severin Grundtvig, who among other things, was an anti-elitist. Grundtvig's beliefs advocated national identity with a sense of belonging. This implied the idea that the Danes shouldn't pursue outer grandeur but seek prosperity in the wellbeing of the people. He also propagated that good living and education should be accessible to everyone equally.

Some anthropologists link this to the Danish welfare state and the high level of equality prevalent. This refers to the difference in wealth and income which is not as pronounced as in other societies. This setup created a sense of security and safety for the people which created a greater focus on home and the notion of being together in a domestic setting.

Another theory about the concept's recent global upsurge compares the work-life balance (or call it imbalance, if you will) of the West to that of the Danes. Many western nations follow a schedule with more work hours in the week, greater workloads to handle, and with very little downtime.

In contrast, the Danish lifestyle supports downtime more and Hygge appears to provide a chance to reclaim that time. Its advent into the western world is fairly recent with Hygge catching on as a lifestyle in the UK in 2016 and then a year later in the US.

Chapter 3: Advantages of Hygge

Hygge may be a centuries-old idea, yet it has become the center of discussion among the majority quite lately. Perhaps the overwhelmingly busy life of this ultra-mechanical era has necessitated the quest for such a stress-alleviating and relaxing phenomenon. This ultra-technological era has made a machine out of the very man for whose benefit these machines were invented. Seeking Hygge is a natural response to the resultant overwhelming pressure of this modern-day busy life.

Hygge is a widely inclusive sentiment of prosperity; a joy got from both physical solaces, and the passionate security of investing energy with friends and family. Hygge is close to home to each person; it tends to taste hot cocoa by a thundering flame while a winter tempest seethes outside or going for a stroll with a companion and visiting about existence. The potential outcomes are tremendous.

Everybody is discussing Hygge nowadays. Hygge is a Danish method for living that generally means comfort. Thus, Hygge is about making your life and home as cozy as could be possible. However, to associate Hygge with coziness and comfort is to conceive it in its narrowest sense. Hygge is not just a simple word or a concept; it's a way of life rather. A way of life that works wonders to enable its followers to transform their day to day simple activities into joyful, pleasant moments of life. Those who can fully comprehend the idea and order their life accordingly, begin to harness the fruits of Hygge quickly.

Hygge is a marvelous phenomenon that enlightens the personal, emotional, psychological and social aspects of human life. Hygge brings peace of mind, security, calmness, comfort, contentment, and relaxation in place of anarchy of mind, insecurity, disturbance, discomfort, discontentment, and hypertension, which are the obvious outcomes of this hectic modern-day life.

Hygge isn't just about inclination cozy; it can help your emotional wellness too.

Denmark (where Hygge is begun from) has been cast a ballot of the most joyful nation on the planet. Elation professionals dependably discover Denmark to have the most cheerful individuals on Earth, which Danes accredit to the practice of Hygge undeniably — feeling expanded joy could be a touch of elbowroom of rehearsing Hygge. In any case, there are so many other emotional, physical, relationship, and psychological benefits as well.

EMOTIONAL BENEFITS

Hygge is primarily centered on inducing a sentiment of calmness and concordance in the living space. Since we grasp the idea, our experiences utilizing our senses of sight, hearing, contact, taste, and smell become more receptive and active to have Hygge. It may stun nobody that the creation of a comfortable living space would empower us to feel less tense and propel a sentiment of passionate thriving and security. These conclusions of comfort and safety can all specifically grant us the space to let down our gatekeeper and be progressively present and open to interfacing with one another.

The fundamental conceivable emotional advantage of HYGGE is that it diminishes pressure, discouragement, and uneasiness. A Hyggelig lifestyle goes a long way in reducing stress, sadness, tension, anxiety or depression, whatever you name it.

Stress is an ever-increasing and universal phenomenon. It is the by-product of this highly technological era which tends to make a machine out of the 'inventor' itself.

Whether it's an outcome of one's inner negative feelings or it's the yield of hostile circumstances, a great deal of pressure can negatively affect your psychological and physical wellbeing. Many psychologist and elation and wellbeing professionals have put forth their solutions to eliminate stress or depression and to promote emotional wellbeing.

Other conceivable emotional advantages include:
- Increased sentiments of self-esteem
- Elevated positive thinking
- A greater feeling of care
- Improved self-sympathy
- Enhanced routine with regards to appreciation

SOCIAL AND RELATIONSHIP BENEFITS

When we feel loved and protected, we will undoubtedly develop and support relationships with others. In a Hygge-centered way of life, there is a much greater emphasis on bonding together with family members and buddies.

Having a strong bonding with the people dearer to us has a very positive effect not only on our sense of personal wellbeing but also on our sense of being a contributor to relationships. We feel continuously sure when related to others, we have a belief that all is well and we can respond to hazards, and we are progressively open to tolerating shortcoming with others, everything that can be supported inside Hygge-style living space.

Instances of conceivable social advantages may include:
• Focus on togetherness
• Feelings of solace and wellbeing
• Increased trust
• Increased closeness
• New social associations
• Improved existing connections
• Less dependence via social-based networking media

Mental health

Here are a few different ways you can grasp Hygge and improve your psychological wellbeing: To be as gainful and sound as could be expected under the circumstances, you need enough great quality rest. Intend to get in any event 8 hours of rest during the evening and take snoozes at whatever point conceivable or required. On the off chance that you need some assistance getting or staying unconscious, have a go at making magnesium or melatonin enhancements to trigger your body's characteristic rest reaction. You can likewise diffuse lavender, organic oil, or rub it on your feet to quiet yourself down before bed. Getting enough rest can enable you to feel your best.

Make a rundown of things that make you feel the most comfortable and agreeable. These things could incorporate candles, warm covers, books, a warm chimney, or quieting music. You could likewise change the lighting in your home. Make tracks in the opposite direction from brilliant, bright lights and spotlight on warm, low lighting.

Hygge is the basic mantra of the Danish. It implies something along the lines of putting your bliss first and making a warm and supporting condition for you.

We feel that the vast majority of us are not kind to ourselves. At whatever point we converse with a companion, discussions comprise of, "we are so worn out. We have never been progressively pushed. We have put on so much weight." The pessimism is alarming. In any case, Hygge gives us to trust. There are such a large number of easily overlooked details in our days that can make us unfathomably cheerful, yet right now, they are muddled in pressure and uneasiness. We have to make an opportunity to stop and enjoy when those things present themselves. Take a gander at the delightful house somewhat more. Exchange viewing Netflix for bringing a once-over to the seashore and light your preferred flame. Clean up. Purchase new blossoms. The most significant thing we can gain from the Danish is that you are the beginning of a world brimming with euphoria. It is ok to deal with yourself first since satisfaction and benevolence to your general surroundings will pursue.

PASSIONATE BENEFITS

Hygge stylistic layout is planned to advance a feeling of quiet and harmony in the living space. Since we understand, our encounters and condition using sight, sound, contact, taste, and smell, it might shock no one that making a comfortable living space would assist us with feeling less restless and advance a feeling of passionate prosperity and wellbeing. This sentiment of solace and wellbeing can all the more likely permit us, and those offering the space to us, to let down our watchmen and be progressively present and open to associating with each other.

Instances of conceivable passionate advantages may include:

- Less sadness and uneasiness
- Expanded sentiments of self-esteem

- Expanded good faith
- Brought down pressure
- More prominent feelings of care
- Developed self-sympathy
- Expanded act of appreciation

Hygge isn't something you can compel: it slips itself into our lives during snapshots of unwinding, where the joy of being a part of an inviting setting is the main thing that matters. Hygge is a feeling, an act of living. Even though it's not something you make, similar to when embellishing a room, there are various methods for consolidating Hygge at home. Along these lines, turn the pot on, put on a woolly sweater, and read on.

Hygge is an art of making intimacy at any moment. Typically, a social event for friends and family to get together to encounter the comradeship, warmth, and happiness of the occasion, it can likewise be appreciated while alone to quiet the nerves and soothe the faculties. It's a thought which breaks climate and natural boundaries. It is something everybody in Denmark shares in, and it has spread through to each part of Scandinavia, enabling the inhabitants of the region to harness the fruits of this amazing concept. Valuing the little delights in life consistently, Hygge followers have taken advantage of a wellspring of satisfaction which the remainder of the world can enormously profit if they perceive the concept and can practice it accordingly.

Chapter 4: How Hygge Helps Happiness

While it is our inalienable right to pursue happiness here in the US, too often it feels elusive considering our hectic, harried lifestyles and attachments to too many material things. Hygge may be one way to right that ship, supported with clear evidence from Denmark being consistently considered the happiest country on earth. Possibly, some guidance from the Hygge lifestyle is just what we need to help guide us to greater happiness.

We all want bliss and happiness, and our ideas of that - and for that - vary from one person to another. For many of us, there are points in our life that disappoint; we thought we were on the path to happiness just to find we weren't even close to the right direction! We wind up very unhappy instead. Many studies have shown that people choosing to follow the high dollar, high-stress careers end up less content than peers who chose rewarding careers helping their fellow man - even if less financially lucrative. This is where a concept like Hygge can come in and reframe our concepts of happiness. Instead of being defined by wealth and achievement, it may be marked by family togetherness and a contented home. If what we once thought we wanted has failed to bring happiness, then surely there are alternate ways of defining happiness. Hygge is demonstrably one of them, as people who practice it routinely report high levels of happiness and contentment.

Happiness as a destination for solely our personal fulfillment should not be the only thing driving us. Living a joyful life is also crucial to our overall health and well-being, emotionally and physically. The medical evidence keeps mounting: unhappiness is detrimental to our short-term needs and our long-term health. Among other things, it promotes heart health. People reporting happiness also report lower blood pressure and heart rates, both of which affect long-term heart health. It also boosts our immune systems; people who consistently maintained positive outlooks on their lives also consistently avoided colds and other minor ailments over time!

Happiness helps us to avoid pain in general - people who claim to be happy report far fewer aches and pains that many of us experience in our daily lives. The difference here may not be necessarily physical, but it is no less powerful to contemplate that our state of mind can alleviate physical pain itself. Other, more complicated diseases have shown to be less severe or to occur less often in people who reported spending a lot of time in social groups. Certainly, high levels of happiness are associated with low levels of stress, and we have all heard of how acutely damaging stress is to our physical well-being over time. Last, happy people often lead longer lives and are more productive well into their later years. The benefits of feeling happiness are undeniable, and, like Hygge, this is a state of mind. The Danes are a great example of Hygge in action!

While happiness is mostly associated with how we feel, it's more than just an emotion. It helps us connect with others and develops our ability to cope when things don't go as we expect. And while most people think that happiness is the absence of negative emotions, it's more of making the most out of any given situation. You see, you can still be happy if your life isn't picture perfect. It's about you doing what you can to have your best life possible.

Happiness is not just a pleasurable feeling, but it's a sense of being the best version of yourself.

Why should happiness matter in our daily lives?

For starters, happy people are healthier. Studies show that people who report being in a happy state of being have stronger immune systems. This means that even if they did get sick, they experienced fewer symptoms and they're able to bounce back faster than those who saw themselves as being anxious, depressed, or angry.

Another benefit that happy people enjoy is that they have rich and meaningful relationships. Let's be real, happy people are just a lot more fun to be with. Would you want to spend your time with someone who sees the world as a bottomless pit? Because happy people are generally more giving and supportive, it's easier for them to make friends. Plus, they're great at maintaining relationships.

Happy people are not just generous when it comes to their material resources, they're very giving of their time and attention as well. They like to volunteer for causes that they feel strongly about, not because they want other people to see how inspiring they are, but because they want to feel like they're making a difference in the grand scheme of things. They help because they also want other people to enjoy the benefits of being happy.

If being happy has all these benefits, why is it that the world lacks happy people? What is it about happiness than makes it so elusive or hard to grasp? According to recent studies, the more you look for happiness, the less likely you will find it.

Think about it for a moment and try to relate it to your experience of searching for happiness. If you're currently the happiest you've ever been, then congratulations to you! But if you're still looking or waiting for it, and most likely you still are, then it might be time to call off the search party.

You see, when you try to pursue happiness, you need to compare it to something to prove that you're making progress. So instead of letting yourself get into the flow of things, you end up evaluating whether the experience is making you happy and to what degree. You become so obsessed with assessing each experience that you forget to enjoy it.

Another reason why you should stop pursuing happiness is that it forces you to define happiness as a strong positive emotion like enthusiasm, excitement, or even joy. The thing is, happiness is not driven by the intensity of the emotion, but the quality of it.

Many wellness experts tout the benefits of the Hygge lifestyle in its improvement over our emotional state of mind, our physical health, and our social well-being. Emotionally, one of the benefits of Hygge is to promote a sense of calm and peacefulness. For example, if your home is cozy and comforting - with gentle candlelit rooms, warm furniture, blankets, and the smells of delicious home cooking - then it stands to reason that your state of mind is also at peace, not stressful. Other emotional benefits of Hygge practice may include a decrease in depression - it's hard to stay depressed when you're comfortable and secure without much anxiety. Additionally, increased feelings of optimism and self-worth are often by-products of practicing Hygge, as your state of mind will not be as linked to external desires and things that may be out of your control. Practicing Hygge in your life leads to physical health benefits. In addition to the emotional benefits, the physical benefits are just as important. Incorporating Hygge into your daily routine can lead to a physically stronger life. For instance, Hygge can improve sleep patterns - crucial to maintaining a sense of calm productivity.

Finally, there are also social benefits gained from practicing Hygge. When we feel safe and comfortable, it becomes easier to reach out to others without feeling insecure and vulnerable. If we make our home welcoming and inviting to ourselves, it follows that others will find out home equally as alluring.

One of the fundamental concepts within Hygge is that togetherness is truly part of the formula for overall happiness. Connecting with others is important both for our well-being and that of our community. This is an art that is being lost in the maze of technological devices and the distractions of our contemporary world. We may like using the word "communication" when discussing our beloved technology of texting or social media, yet our devices don't foster an authentic sense of connection. Hygge can help us to regain some of that feeling of connection. Achieving happiness through Hygge involves focusing on creating a cozy space and a comforting lifestyle; this facilitates and nurtures happier feelings. For example, if your home is a space of refuge - a calm, shared space with a warm fire, decorated with soothing natural materials - then you are likely to feel protected, safe, and calm.

Don't limit yourself to practicing Hygge just in your home or on your days off. This is a lifestyle that takes time to cultivate, carrying with it the worthwhile goal of improving your happiness, health, and well-being. Implement some of these strategies at your place of employment when possible and appropriate. Reflect on the benefits of walking into an office with soft lighting, personal and pleasant pictures, with perhaps a plant of two. That office is infinitely more inviting than one with harsh overhead lights and nothing more personal than a desktop computer. Think about a mental health professional's office; most are purposefully designed to comfort and soothe the patients who enter there. This can also be your purpose at work, putting clients or others at ease as well as lowering your own levels of stress.

Think about other ways to cultivate the Hygge spirit throughout your daily activities. Communing with nature, rather than zoning out with our technological devices, is one sure way to practice the habit of Hygge. Take a leisurely bike ride and walk along the trails to experience the natural world; be present and unhurried in how you approach activity. The goal is to feel calm and peaceful, not frantic and competitive. Slow down a bit: the contemporary American lifestyle is geared to go at lightning speed, and this often means we miss out on the little joys, such as listening to birdsong or watching a sunset. You can also think of Hygge as a way to do good in the world, albeit in small, incremental ways. Practice sustainability for the greater common good. Recycling, eating locally produced foods, and seeking out environmentally friendly power sources are all activities that adhere to the overall spirit of Hygge.

You can also carry Hygge with you throughout your day via your attitude, your way of presenting yourself, your way of connecting with others - even strangers. In the next chapter, we will explore the many little things that can make up our peaceful day while practicing Hygge.

Chapter 5: Hygge Principles

MINDFULNESS AND THE SENSES

Mindfulness may be the hardest principle on the list, yet it is one of the most important to cultivate your true happiness through this practice. Mindfulness means you are paying attention to the moment. You are fully engaged in whatever activity you are immersed in presently.

Here are some common situations that you can practice being more mindful of what you're doing:

- Watching a movie
- Reading a book
- Having a conversation with a friend
- Drinking a cup of tea

Mindfulness refers to any moment in your life where you are absorbed in the moment, enjoying yourself, and not worrying about the past or the future. Mindfulness is a habit you must develop over time. You can't expect yourself to always be mindful; you have to constantly work on it. One great way to achieve mindfulness is to simply stop what you are doing a minute or two each day and savor the world around you. Take this time to breathe in deeply and truly process what you're seeing, hearing, feeling, and doing. When you are engrossed in a task and realize your mind is wandering, pull it back to the present. Redirect your thoughts to the present moment until it becomes a habit for you to think in this manner.

GRATITUDE AND BEING POSITIVE

It may seem like common sense that looking at the positive side of things would make us feel happier, but that doesn't mean it is an easy practice. we may not even realize that we are being negative sometimes.

Think and act positively in all you do. Choose to talk about the good things instead of complaining. Look for sources of good news instead of overwhelming yourself and feeling down about all the tragedies around the world. It is important to be informed, but not to the point that you feel depressed due to dark and gloomy headlines. You do not have to think about bad news 24/7 to stay in touch with what's happening globally and locally.

NATURE

Nature is what we come from, physically and spiritually. Even if modern conveniences make our lives easier, there is still a part within each of us that summons the wild. Nature is a great way to practice using all your senses as well. Smelling flowers, feeling the cold chill of the wind on your cheek, listening to birds singing, and seeing the bright colors of spring can inspire anyone's appreciation and encourage them to love the world around him or her.

EASE AND COMFORT

This is something that can easily be expressed through what you wear or how things are done in your home. One of the words used to describe the word Hygge is "cozy," and that is what you are trying to achieve. Surround yourself with things that bring you comfort and warmth.

Try these ideas for keeping things comfortable in your home and in your life:

- Use pillows that are soft, comfortable, and minimalistic, instead of flashy and impractical ones.
- Wear your favorite sweatpants and a comfortable sweater for the day instead of dressing up.
- Go makeup-free when you feel like it.
- Keep soft slippers available for use indoors.

- Remember, comfort and ease go hand-in-hand, so the comfortable choices you make should not be challenging or difficult ones.
- Choose to abandon the discomforts of life if you can. You can't always avoid discomfort since it is an inevitable part of life, but sometimes you endure uncomfortable things because you choose to do so. You don't have to! If you have a pair of shoes that look nice but feel horrible, donate. You don't need to sacrifice comfort for temporary beauty.

If there is someone around you who makes you uncomfortable or radiates a negative presence, don't feel as if you have to keep this person in your life. If talking it over doesn't work, it's better to free yourself from that negativity and bad influence and focus on the people who bring happiness and comfort to your life. You should evaluate people that you don't like or don't want to be around and remove them if you can.

Making life easier does not make you lazy; it makes you smart. If you find a way to streamline work or automate your technology, then do so. You are busy and tired enough—why add stress to your life by doing things the hard way? Remember, comfort and ease are important factors in your new lifestyle.

TOGETHERNESS

The Danish believe in spending quality time with one another. Friends and loved ones should take up a good portion of your time, even if it feels difficult to make time in your busy schedule. Don't you feel better after a cup of coffee with your best friend or a Netflix night with your spouse? There is a reason for that. We are all connected, and we are all meant to complement one another. You cannot have true happiness without taking advantage of companionship.

One of the major principles of this time spent with those you care for relates to mindfulness. It means giving your full attention to the people that you are with currently. Cell phones and other distractions can keep you distant and only allow you to experience part of the moment. These should be set aside in favor of conversations and physical closeness. Stop letting insignificant distractions get in the way of truly being there with your loved ones.

PLEASURE

Can you honestly say that you do that regularly? You may take a vacation or two every year and make time for a fancy date night once a month, but Hygge principles embody something even simpler than that. Hygge pleasure is about slowing down and enjoying the small things that you don't have to look far to find. This could be your favorite dessert, a walk along the beach with the feeling of sand in between your toes, or the laughter of your children as you tickle them. We need to learn to find these moments and make them happen. Pleasure in a Hygge lifestyle is about the experience around us, instead of unexpected lavish gifts and large expensive events.

MINIMALISM AND QUIET

Part of Hygge is the belief that minimalism will bring you peace and happiness. This mentality applies to every facet of life, but especially regarding your home décor. Having the bare minimum that you need in furniture with a simple layout, including a quiet corner to have some time alone to read or meditate, can make you feel less cluttered.

Excess amounts of stuff can stress you out and bog down your energy. You have too many things to worry about, organize, and clean. There is no need for so much clutter. Having a more minimal lifestyle allows you to breathe, both literally and metaphorically.

Consider donating things instead of throwing them away haphazardly. The act of being kind to others can give you a warm sense of pleasure, which is all part of Hygge.

HYGGE PITFALLS

Although the principles listed above may sound easy, they can be more challenging than you may realize. Be aware of these potential mistakes and pitfalls that could hinder your Hygge attempts:

Spending too much time on yourself. Although helping yourself feel better and reducing stress in your life is a big part of Hygge, you should also make time for your friends, pets, colleagues, and family members. Hygge is about making yourself comfortable as well as increasing the comfort of those around you. It's also about learning to love yourself and others more, and about expressing that love and appreciation, too.

Spending too much money. You may be tempted to throw out everything you own to replace it with more minimalistic furnishings and items, but that isn't very practical and can make you more stressed and anxious. If you're already trying to practice Hygge on a budget, this can be even more upsetting and difficult. Even if you're not on a budget, there's no need to waste the items you already have. Instead, you may want to just remove some of the items in your home while keeping those you can use. Remember that Hygge needs to be functional and practical to work.

Unrealistic expectations. Hygge works slowly, over time, to improve your mood and help you feel good. It will not immediately solve all your problems with your job, relationships, or life in general. Go into it expecting to work to achieve those goals, rather than looking for a magical fix. Even with lots of time, Hygge may not solve every issue in your life. This concept is not meant to be a quick solution, but rather a lifestyle change that can help you learn to face problems and work through difficulties more easily. Be sure you're approaching Hygge with a healthy mindset to get the most out of it.

Be on the lookout for these pitfalls when you first get started with Hygge and later on in your practice, too. These issues can appear at any time throughout your Hygge experience, but they can be easily avoided when you're prepared to potentially deal with them. If you're practicing Hygge with others in your life, then you can help each other look out for signs of these hazards, too.

Chapter 6: How to Make Hygge Part of Your Life

You know you need to adapt two areas of your life to adopt the Hygge lifestyle. You will need to make your home Hygge, and you will need to change your social gatherings to be more relaxing and comfortable.

What are some steps you can take on right now to ensure this happens?

WRITE OUT YOUR GOALS.

People who write their goals down can refer to those goals when life gets too tough or gets in the way. It is also a way for you to truly commit because it is like you are signing a contract with yourself when you write down your goals.

START EFFECTING CHANGE IN ONE AREA OF YOUR LIFE

It is suggested that you start with one room in your home. Make it Hygge. If necessary, change the furniture, paint, wall décor, and remove the clutter. Add plush pillows, soft blankets, favorite books, and even a fireplace if you can.

Once your first room is Hygge, start spending ten minutes to an hour in this space per week. You are actively saying you will be comfortable and simple for a few minutes to an hour. You will start to feel the happiness return and the stress fall away. You will desire to spend more time in this area to the point that you will start setting aside more time to enjoy the cozy, comfortable space.

Work in each room of your home, until it is streamlined, uncluttered, and relaxing. You may need to eliminate some of the things you own. Materialistic natures will not work with Hygge unless you leave one space for your cluttered needs. The overall aim should be to eliminate as much as you can that makes you feel pressured. For example, if you never have time for the things you bought like exercise videos, video games, or other things, then get rid of them. There is no reason to keep the clutter if you have forgotten it exists.

Now that you have your home in the Hygge way, you can enjoy any room. Perhaps on Monday, you decide to enjoy hot chocolate in front of the fire while reading a good book. On Wednesday, you decide to have family night where you spend an hour at the dinner table before everyone goes their separate ways. You do not want to schedule these evenings but simply enjoy them.

GET TOGETHER (WITH JUST A FEW CLOSE FRIENDS)

The social association is the best indicator of our endless bliss. Harmony is a focal precept of Hygge and the foundation at which many other Hygge standards and exercises are based. Be that as it may, Hygge mingling isn't about enormous, lavish gatherings. Or maybe, it is in the organization of a couple of dear companions in a domain of trust, solace, and security.

ENJOY GOOD FOOD AND DRINK

A Hygge sustenance experience is pleasant and warm. It is easygoing, natural, and moderate. This experience can be delighted in at home or at your preferred bistro, café, or bar (or whatever another foundation where the environment is comfortable, and the music isn't unreasonably noisy for discussion).

Hygge sustenance is a liberal stew, freshly warmed bread, a warm fire seared cheddar with soup, or a common bowl of popcorn. The Danes additionally love their desserts, particularly preparing and eating cakes, treats, and cakes. Anything home-cooked is considerably more Hygge than something locally acquired.

Hygge refreshments are best served warm. Tea, hot cocoa, and considered wine all have a high Hygge factor. Especially on a freezing winter night, yet the Danes' most cherished Hygge drink is hot espresso. Gradually tasting liquor is likewise connected with Hygge. This could be drinking a glass of red wine while a tempest seethes outside or getting a charge out of a glass of bourbon or Irish coffee around the pit fire. Meeting up with companions at an agreeable parlor or speakeasy gets the Hygge going also.

DETACH AND SAVOR THE MOMENT

You can't achieve Hygge while perusing your phone or email. Hygge is connected to isolating and getting a charge out of the present moment. It is shared encounters straightforwardly at the current time, taking it all in without imagining being somewhere else. Seek after the Danes' lead by leaving wear down the time and returning home to eat and playout and out. Your email and electronic interpersonal interaction toward the weekend (and irrefutably when you're on a trip) prevent you from enjoying the moment. Hygge life is central and moderate. Go disengaged to turn the Hygge on.

TURN THE LIGHTS DOWN LOW

A Hygge situation is lessened and low, not light and breathtaking. The perfect Hygge lighting is practiced by making a fire, turning on low-temperature lights, or lighting two or three candles. Hygge light is the first hour of sunrise or the latest hour of sunset. Go outside for that magical experience or endeavor to imitate that level of lighting inside. At the point when all is said to be done, you're going for the light of flares, not fluorescents.

GET OUT IN NATURE – REJUVENATE YOURSELF

Though the home is much of the time where the Hygge is, it is created outside too. Hygge is normal, bright, and country, many equivalents to nature. Gravitate toward life, and you will encounter Hygge.

It could be a ski trip with mates, a significant move in the forested territories, an outside excursion, or even just a walk around the square. Circle yourself with nature — on a vessel, at a buddy's hotel, seeing the dusk, or looking toward the stars — and let the Hygge wash over you.

If you live in an urban setting, you can search out an open park, waterway, or network nursery to draw nearer to nature. Walk or bicycle to work if that is an alternative or take a walk each day on your mid-day break. Having a pooch will likewise prompt a lot of strolls outside (also friendship).

SELF-INDULGENCE

Devote some time to YOU – the center of your world! Another ideal time to Hygge: On vacation, that is a definite opportunity to abandon your obligations regarding a couple of days. Furthermore, there's no better spot to experience its pressure busting benefits than in the nation – and city – where Hygge is woven into the texture of everyday life.

MESS AROUND AND GET CREATIVE

Consider fun traditions that you can start with friends and family. There are a great deal of financial and clear ways to discover Hygge if you're willing to endeavor new things. Maybe it is a family game night every Friday or inviting buddies over once every month for film and popcorn night. Or then again, maybe only an everyday practice of unwinding on the love seat and viewing your preferred TV show toward the finish of a taxing week.

Rather than eating out, have a go at having companions over for a potluck supper where everybody brings a dish, or consider beginning cooking or wine sampling club that meets consistently. You could moreover have a dear partner over for espresso or tea constantly — if there is a warm fire and some fragile music far out, even better.

CELEBRATE THE SEASONS

It ought not to stun anybody that winter is the most Hygge season, and Christmas is the most Hygge event of all.

Handle it by being with close family and colleagues, watching event movies, setting up improvements, and getting a charge out of incredible sustenance and drink. Go ice skating or sledding, and warm up with hot cocoa by the fire. Sit by the window and watch the snowfall outside.

HYGGE IN THE GYM

With all this talk about coziness and snuggling up, it's easy to believe that Hygge is a lazy person's match. However, exercise is very Hygge -- it is about producing warmth, feeling the best you can feel, even physically, and maximizing your potential for self-indulgence. Wear gym clothing that you feel comfortable in is vital, and if you are an outdoor runner, a sports gilet may be the very best thing that you by this season. Most importantly, exercise is intended to allow you to feel great, so be certain to reward yourself after hitting the gym!

The feeling of Hygge is a warm and comfy one. It is the way we feel if we are tucked up hot while it is stormy out or the feeling of a hot cup in our palms. It is laughing with family and friends by candlelight along with the gratification of a gut filled with fantastic food and beverage. It's simple to know why this sort of attitude to lifestyle is indeed significant to this Danish. Denmark has a harsh and cold climate, but still has good all-natural beauty. Having the ability to associate with this setting whilst maintaining relaxation is exactly what Hygge is about.

What is so amazing about Hygge is that it is something that we can all incorporate into our daily lives. It is about taking the time to delight in the things, people and places that you love, whether this means taking some time during your lunch break to go for a walk outside or finishing your day with a warm cup of tea and a novel instead of scrolling endlessly through Instagram. We can all afford more times such as these today. In today's civilization, the accomplishments and hard work are often prioritized, and as significant as these items are, it's easy to forget that people also ought to take the time to relax and revel in the present. After all, that is we have worked so hard for.

COOK SOME HYGGE FOOD

Hygge food is simple and comforting, close to nature and far from pre-packaged. Most of the eatables are preferably prepared at home whether sweet or savory. Typical Danish favorites can include anything from home-baked bread, muffins, and pastries to aromatic tea, and spiced wine.

At its best, Hygge food will remind you of pleasant childhood memories with invigorating breakfasts, addicting snacks, hearty soups, comforting entrees and decadent desserts. It is a time when family and friends come together over home-cooked meals.

The joy of eating comes from enjoying your food, focusing on the sensations of smell, flavors and textures. Eating this way also means none of the yoyo dieting trends, extreme detoxes or cutting out entire food groups. Instead, seek out flavor over calorie counting or portion control and balance it out with regular activity. Hygge food should be a treat and not concerned with the limits of healthy nutrition. Instead, it is a welcome diversion from healthy eating.

Comfort food is quintessentially Hygge. This is food that warms the soul, evokes happiness, awakens the taste buds and brings back memories of childhood. And it's not just the food itself, but the way you enjoy it with friends and family which lends it the Hygge factor.

ADOPT THE LIGHT

To offer your distance that tranquil Hygge atmosphere, concentrate on creating the best lighting. Make the most of natural light when possible - pulling the blinds up, setting a seat by a window bask to bask in its stunning glow. Since Denmark has long and dark winters, man-made lighting integrated, through overhead fittings and unscented candles.

COMMUNITY

Community plays a massive part in Hygge since it is believed that life's feel-good comforts are heightened in the company of friends. You can apply this to any range of actions: from watching a film and sipping coffee by a fire or hiking in the forests to just reading a book beside somebody else.

SAVOR THE FLAVORS

Hygge involves all five senses, so food should not be overlooked. Warm beverages like coffee, tea, and glögg (Scandinavian mulled wine) as well as hearty dishes like pie, pastries, and porridge can help you attain the greatest Hygge. Additionally, it binds to the notion of community: food and drinks taste better when appreciated by loved ones as well!

HYGGE AT WORK

Most businesses will ban lit candles in the office (as it is a fairly obvious fire hazard) but they may be alright with the use of a subtle infuser. Smell is intrinsically connected to mood; therefore adorable White Company diffusers might be the difference between a fantastic day and a terrible one. Another essential facet of Hygge is maintaining warmth, keeping a warm water bottle on your table is great for beating the workplace chill. Finally, even the most evil companies allow you to keep your nearest and dearest, so take advantage of this and invest in frames that can do justice to your favorite pictures.

SLOW DOWN

Your cooking, that is, the more drawn out something takes to cook, the more Hygge it is. That doesn't mean going through hours julienning vegetables and making muddled coatings — we're talking taking as much time as is needed, not ripping your hair out. A dish chicken, a pot of stew, some warming soup — basic; however, heavenly nourishment is critical. Even better, welcome your companions over and isolate the heap. Preparing dinner to share is about more or less Hyggelig.

BENEFIT A FEW

Helping other people has been scientifically proven to add to your very own bliss. In Copenhagen, you'll see numerous activities to support supportability, regardless of whether its natural eateries, solar controlled vessels or associations like Too Good to go, a Danish application that causes you to discover cafés close to you that have sworn to help battle food squander.

LIGHT SOME CANDLES

Light Some Candles. Ask any Danish individual, and they'll reveal to you that the least demanding approach to make a Hyggelig air is with candles. Danes experience a larger number of candles than some other country on earth – an astounding 13 pounds of flame wax per individual every year. They even utilize the expression "lyselukker," which signifies "somebody who puts out the candles," to allude to a spoilsport.

LIGHT A FIRE

If a candle is comfortable, a fire is much cozier. It feels considerably more fun to watch a real fire than to have light and warmth conveyed to you through electric bulbs. In the late spring, you can accumulate around an open-air fire in an outside fire pit – lasting or convenient. In any event, cooking supper over a fire allows you to watch the blazes and possibly toast a couple of marshmallows.

In the winter, in case you're not fortunate enough to have an indoor chimney, do the following best thing and stream a video of a snapping fire on your TV. You can't feel the warmth, however, you can watch the blazes gleam and hear the logs pop. There are free chimney recordings accessible on YouTube that run for three to 10 hours.

PUT ON COMFY CLOTHES

It is extremely unlikely to feel extremely comfortable while wearing a tailored suit. To get Hygge, you have to change into something simple and agreeable. Overwhelming sweaters and sewed socks are great decisions for wintertime since they keep you warm, which is basic to the Hygge state of mind. A couple of Hyggebusker (sweats or different jeans you'd never wear in broad daylight) complete the outfit.

GO FOR A STROLL

Danes love to take long strolls in a wide range of climate – regardless, winter or summer. Strolling is particularly Hyggelig when you do it with a companion or a gathering of companions. It's an opportunity to talk and appreciate each other's conversation without spending a penny. However, in any event, going for a stroll without anyone else, or with your canine, is an approach to draw nearer to nature and enjoy a reprieve from a bustling calendar.

RIDE A BIKE

Bikes are mainstream in Denmark. Denmark.dk, the country's legitimate site, says the capital city of Copenhagen is known for its cycling society and is perceived as the principal official Bike City on the planet. Bicycles are Hygge because they move at a slower pace than vehicles, allowing you to appreciate the view.

On the off chance that you effectively possess a bicycle, think about cycling to work. Various investigations show that individuals who bicycle to work are both more beneficial and more joyful than individuals who drive. On the off chance that you don't have one, check whether you can get one used. Locales like Craigslist and eBay frequently have essential models in great condition for $100 or less. Another choice is to join a bicycle sharing system if your city has one. Submit a general direction to the Danes and get in the seat. Visit Copenhagen, and you'll see it isn't only a bicycle benevolent city; it's a bicycle commanded one. You'll see a more significant number of bikes than autos in the inside, and 350km of cycleways and paths secure the town. How does cycling help up your Hygge? It drives you to back off and take in your environment. "You can see and alternately detect individuals when you're on a bicycle," says Jeppe Linnet, an anthropologist who looks into Hygge.

CREATE A HYGGEKROG

While the entire home is done up to look and feel Hyggeligt with natural fibers, soft lighting, warm hues, and cozy accessories, a Hyggekrog is a special nook within the Hygge home. You can create your own cozy place where you can do simple things such as enjoy a hot cup of cocoa, read, knit or even watch the sun go down. This place can be as luxurious or as simple as you want it to be.

While typically, Hygge is a social occasion for loved ones to get together to experience camaraderie, warmth and contentment, it can also be enjoyed alone to calm the nerves and soothe the senses.

Keep your Hyggekrog clean and simple, resisting the urge to overstuff it with furnishing and accessories. Since it is a place where you wish to sit and unwind, keeping it warm yet minimal will help you relax better.

GET DELICATE

A large home isn't just about what things resemble, yet how they feel. Hygge incorporates a notion of solace and comfort, and you can help it alongside a piece by altering your condition to be more Hyggelig. Pick covers, hurls, and cushions in material surfaces that you can nestle under.

DRESS IN COMFORTABLE CLOTHING

Comfort is an important element of Hygge. If you look at the aesthetics of Hygge, you'll find that comfortable clothing is always there. Think of oversized sweaters, thick, warm socks and scarves and stretchy loungewear when contemplating Hygge attire.

This is clothing that doesn't restrict movement, allows you to shift positions freely, and there is none of the pull-down-your-hemline or keep fixing a shifting neckline. Fancy but uncomfortable clothing can make you sit and stay painfully still because you feel conscious of what you have worn. You get to dress up for specific occasions, but we're only talking about when at home and among people you have no reservations from.

BE HERE AT THIS POINT

Be in the present, not adhered to what's happening on the web. "It isn't such a lot of that electronic contraptions are limited from Hygge, yet all things considered, it would mean saving them and being as one for quite a while without them," says Linnet. In this way, concerning contributing vitality with your friends and family, agree to avoid the phones for an hour or two.

CREATE EXTRAORDINARY OUT OF THE ORDINARY

Hygge is more than a passing extravagance for Danes, rather it's a way of thinking that structures an essential piece of their interminable achievement on the planet joy diagrams - and it could be your antitoxin to the pressure of present-day life. It is calming everything down. Hygge is about simple delights throughout everyday life. Great food and great companions are encompassing it. It is taking it all in and appreciating the occasion. It is a satisfaction out of the ordinary. It is doing some incredible things for the Danes, and I trust it works for you, as well.

Chapter 7: Stress, Hygge, and Mindfulness

Anxiety is a daily issue for many people. The minute we wake up until we go to bed, we're always hurrying to get from place to place, combating traffic, fighting to meet deadlines, and trying to finish everything on our to-do lists. This constant struggle takes its toll on our physical and psychological health and can result in numerous disorders and disorders.

Reducing stress and anxieties also promotes mental health. Many cases of depression, including the seasonal variety, can be traced back to an overflow of cortisol in the body, specifically for those who suffer from chronic migraines that create lesions in the brain that hamper neurotransmitter receptors. Lesions prevent those synapses and neurons from absorbing the chemicals the brain needs to balance itself. This imbalance results in a slew of issues, all because of an overload of cortisol in response to constant stressors.

Emotional health is also impacted by the lifestyle of Hygge. All of these issues that stem from debilitated physical and mental health ultimately affect someone emotionally. Chemical imbalances can create mood swings that lead to mounting self-consciousness, anxiety and panic attacks. These attacks promote more bodily harm, which in turn causes a negative reel of thoughts to play out repeatedly in someone's head, and the cyclical process ultimately destroys all three facets of personal health. This happens all because of a chronic surge of cortisol in their systems.

Commonly, a social event where family members get together to enjoy the comradeship, warmth and contentment of this occasion can also calm the nerves and soothe the senses. An idea that not only breaches seasonal and weather obstacles but also avoids social media, it's something everybody in Denmark partakes in. Furthermore, it's spread to each component of living to be part of their national awareness.

You do not have to completely re-evaluate your home to make it more Hyggeligt; miniature additions into the house can change any time. Allowing yourself to drink your favorite coffee, relaxing in a fresh bubble bath by candlelight or ultimately placing your favorite photographs on the walls are instant mood lifters if you take the opportunity to appreciate them.

Finding new hobbies to enjoy at the house lets you turn off and calms the brain. Switch off the TV and instead, appreciate something fresh you could cultivate throughout your Hygge time in the house or pick up an old hobby that you used to enjoy but stopped doing.

We're constantly hurrying, are not we? We always have someplace to be and we're constantly considering another thing we must do whilst doing something else. To genuinely Hygge, you must slow down a little to take everything in. There will always be something to think about or worry about. However, Hygge teaches you to consider every moment as it is, without hurrying onto another. Simply take an opportunity to relish the cup of coffee you've made, take an additional ten minutes in the tub to ensure worries have faded away, and savor that piece of cake - or you may regret it afterward.

Hygge preferences aren't about wowing or impressing guests – instead, they are about developing a warm and inviting setting that family and friends never wish to leave. Dinners do not have to be styled to perfection with a ten-course tasting menu and celebrations do not require a lengthy list of cocktails followed by a private DJ - take parties back to fundamentals for a more organic, pleasing feel.

The important notion behind Hygge is to delight in the surroundings around you and this is the most important idea for your house. Each room should be a refuge to sink into at any given time and therefore full of key items to permit you to achieve this. Because of increasingly stressful lifestyles, an urgency is put on the requirement to 'escape' the normal to experience true comfort. Hygge fights against this idea by demonstrating that general wellbeing could be improved by making little modifications to regular surroundings, relieving the requirement to escape in any way. Therefore, whatever you're doing, take the opportunity to relish the small moments which make you smile and uplift your spirit. Whilst Hygge is often connected with coziness, it's a means of life that may be enjoyed at any time.

Be as true to yourself as possible. Be yourself. Your actual self. Let your shield fall away and expose who you are. You will not be assaulted on Hygge turf and should also never strike somebody else in return. As soon as we strip ourselves of attempting to establish something that we are not, we can all connect in a far more genuine way. Competition, whether it involves boasting or pretense, isn't bonding, but instead subtly divides us from each other by creating an air of superiority and disdain.

Forget about the controversies that plague modern life. If your chosen topic of conversation is too severe, divisive or controversial, it's likely is not Hyggeligt. Hygge is all about a balanced ebb and flow of conversation in a light-hearted manner. The attention is on the present time and being present at the moment you are living with those around you. We have got plenty of time in our own daily lives to wax poetic on our political opinions and debate and pretend we are experts on everything around us. However, Hygge is all about loving the food you are eating, the organization rather than getting caught up in things that eliminate that. Thus, whining, heavy burdens, guesswork are therefore prohibited from the Hygge area.

A Hygge area is a place in which everyone can relax and state what plagues their hearts without fearing the consequences, regardless of what is happening in their lives at the time. For better or for worse, this particular area is sacred and issues could be left out. This is unique as it allows for friends and families to always be able to speak their minds and show their true selves within this area without the fear of judgment.

Chapter 8: How to Create Your Own Hygge Home

Your home should be neat, tidy, clean, and be filled with homemade items to be Hygge. You may not have a fireplace, but there are now heaters that offer a fake fireplace, with warmth that can bring about the cozy feeling of a fireplace in your home. Bringing the outdoors is about keeping plants in your home that offer new oxygen and fragrance to your rooms.

You may not like to read or drink hot chocolate; however, there are probably activities you do like that are simple. The Hygge lifestyle is about taking the time to relax, whether you enjoy a nap for an hour or listening to relaxing music.

The main part of bringing Hygge into your home is ensuring that the décor and atmosphere is relaxing and cozy to you. This may require you to change your home completely to make it comfortable. It may be necessary for you to change your thoughts on what is relaxing.

Home decorators believe there certain colors or tones should be in a home to provide a cozy, comfortable feeling. You may want to strip a room down to the walls, repaint in a soft blue, grey, or other color decorators suggest. The color needs to be more of an outdoor color or one that gives you a sense of peace. Most people who have light earth tones enjoy their inside space because it feels like the outdoors. However, when the earth tones are too dark it becomes depressing and the room can feel closed in.

When it comes to celebrating Hygge, work on creating a home atmosphere that you can be happy and comfortable with. If you are not able to go home and feel relieved from all the hassle that is going on in your life, you aren't able to find comfort anywhere. The good news is that everyone can work on their homes differently. You will not head to Denmark and find all of the homes are looking exactly the same. Some features help to add to the Hyggelig home, but these are not necessarily requirements, and you can pick and choose the ones that you would like to use. Some of the things that you can do to turn your home into a Hyggelig home include:

USE SOME CANDLES

Many of the Danish countries have found that the warm glow that comes from candles can be relaxing and comforting. Think of how comfortable you are when you gather around a big fire with your friends and family; the candle can give that kind of the same feeling inside of your home. When it is time to relax, rather than relying on all the harsh lights that are around your home, you can learn to rely on some candles to give you the light that you need.

ADD IN SOME MORE TEXTURE

If you want to make sure that the interior of your home is warm and cozy, you will want to add in some nice warm textures to the home. The more textures that you have in the home, think about the chunky cushions, fluffy rugs, throws on the couches, can help to add a bit more coziness and hominess to you and others who come into your home. These textured accessories are a bit trendy in the Danish countries right now, and they can help to make the home look more inviting. When you combine them with some of the nice candlelight or even a fireplace, you will find that everyone who enters your home will have a sense of Hygge.

THE SIMPLE THINGS

You will not be responsible for completely redoing the whole house when it comes to taking on Hygge in the home. Remember that Hygge is different for everyone and it is what makes you feel comfortable, not someone else, so design the home and pick out the items that make you feel the best inside of your own home.

CHILLING OUT WITH FRIENDS

Hygge is all about being social. It is not an event where you sit at home and ignore the world. Yes, there are days when you are tired and just need a break and there are days when you just want to hang out at home with your spouse and your kids and this is just fine. But humans are social creatures and pretending that we don't want to be around anyone else or that we don't like company can cause a lot of harm to our bodies. We need to be around others and we aren't able to feel complete and happy and experience the full extent of Hygge if we don't spend time with others.

TAKE UP A NEW HOBBY

While a good deal of Hygge involves being social with others, it also allows for some time for yourself. Taking up a new hobby can help you to refocus your mind on some of those hard days and gives you a way to get away from that television before it takes over your life. When you take up a hobby, you will learn how to do something new that will help you grow during this time.

LEARN HOW TO BE YOURSELF

The most important thing that you can do with Hygge is learning how to be yourself. If you are pretending that you are someone else or not showing your true self to the others who are around you, you will find that it is hard to be comfortable with some of the others that are around you. And when you don't feel comfortable, it is hard to experience the Hygge that you are looking for.

ENJOY THE ENVIRONMENT THAT YOU ARE IN

One of the big ideas that come with Hygge is to learn how to enjoy the environment that you are in right now. This can be anywhere that you go. But the first place to start is in the home. You should make sure that all of the rooms in your home are sanctuaries that you can enjoy when they are needed. You should make sure that all of the rooms in your home are filled with the items that you need to feel relaxed and safe.

USE HYGGE ALL OF THE TIME.

This way of life is not something that you just experience at night, on weekends, or during the holidays. It is a feeling that you can have all day and every day. You can make your home fit into one of the sanctuaries for Hygge so you can relax from the world after work. You can go and hang out with some friends outside on a walk or at the park. You can take some time to enjoy a cool drink and a book when you need to relax, or even enjoying that cup of coffee before getting the day started.

This is an experience that you will be able to bring with you to all of the different times of your life, you just need to learn to add in some of the social aspects of your life, learn how to relax and enjoy what is going on, and just enjoy some of the little things in your life, and you will find that Hygge can be around you all the time.

Chapter 9: Hygge your Workplace

Wherever you work, there is an opportunity to embrace Hygge even in the most unusual situations. Here are several ways to Hygge your personal workspace. From the office to a construction site, you can extend the feeling of comfort that Hygge embraces.

LUNCH

Do you find all your coworkers drift off to the staff canteen or use their lunch hour to do other things? Why not encourage them to bring in dishes from home and then host a potluck at work. The Danish believe that sharing food is the perfect way to Hygge and by taking this concept to work, you are making it a Hygge environment. Tasting each other's dishes and sharing recipes is a great way to connect with your fellow workers.

SOCIAL SUPPORT

Be nicer to other people. It's as simple as that. You could bring in a coffee for your fellow workers or lend them a stapler. Kindness is sometimes seen as a weakness but, in reality, random acts of kindness can relieve stress both for the recipient and the giver.

TAKE A BREAK

Whenever you can take a breath of fresh air, leave the building and have a stroll. Take a quick walk around the block or a nearby park. Take five minutes to sit on a bench and appreciate your surroundings. If the weather is bad, then take a coat or umbrella. When you spend all day cooped up and the only outside space you see is the walk to your workplace or to your car, then you can feel jaded and claustrophobic but getting outdoors will help you unwind and return to work feeling regenerated.

FAVORITE MUG

Most people love coffee or tea at work and, even in summer, a caffeine boost is needed to increase energy levels. When you have a mug that reminds you of home, you are creating a relaxed atmosphere at work. If you don't have caffeine and stick to soft drinks, bring in your favorite glass. The idea is to bring a piece of home to the office.

NATURAL MATERIALS

If you have the chance, surround yourself with objects that are composed of natural materials. Your desk could be a great starting point. If you have a choice, choose a solid wooden desk that looks classic and comforting. Modern chipboard desks are not inspiring and merely serve a function. No choice but modern? No problem just make sure you have a simple wooden bowl or something similar to look at when you are working.

AFTER WORK BONDING

Hygge is a feeling of belonging and being surrounded by the familiar and since we spend so much time at work, it makes sense to get to know workmates. Organize outings after work and get to know your colleagues. You can learn a lot over a shared beer! Having fun together will lead to better relationships and then you can all Hygge together!

MAKING THE SPACE YOUR OWN

One of the best things that you can use when it comes to making sure that you bring some Hygge into the workspace is to make it your own. You won't be able to bring everything you have at home into the workspace, but when you spend some time making the area a bit homier, it will be easier to get work done and feel good about your work.

MAKE SOME FRIENDS AT WORK

When you go to work, what are some of the things that you do? You probably show up at the last minute, early in the morning, and then try to get to work. But how many interactions do you have at the workplace, especially when it comes to your other coworkers? Unless you are forced to talk to them, do you get a chance to interact with and meet some of the coworkers who are in the same building as you?

Chapter 10: Cultivate the Hygge Mindset

Cultivating the Hygge mindset involves an internal recognition of this lifestyle. For those who are successful in adapting Hygge, the process starts in the heart. The focus shifts from attaining outward perfection to inward comfort and security.

Let me explain this a little. Our modern-day society demands perfection on so many levels; a perfect home, a perfect family, perfect kids, the perfect job, the perfect relationship, the perfect body weight and shape, you name it. It entices individuals to be perfect to be acceptable. Anything less than perfect resonates failure.

And as you can see, all these perfectionist demands are outcome-oriented rather than process-oriented. We aim for the perfect body and weight so that we look good in whatever we decide to wear, and people complement us. We aim for the perfect job so that we can make more money and get complemented on our success. We want perfect kids so that everyone can complement our parenting skills. And the greater glory lies in external recognition rather than internal satisfaction.

But when you decide to Hygge instead, personal satisfaction comes first. Rather than have your living room replicate a glamorous magazine cover, you will wish for it to be a safe sanctuary for yourself and your loved ones. Instead of going to social gatherings where you know no one, you will prefer to meet up with your close friends to have a good time. And instead of going out to eat every weekend, you would rather prepare a hearty homecooked meal to enjoy with your family and kids while perhaps playing a board game together.

All these simple pleasures will bring you greater joy, comfort and reassurance. there is no better way to self-indulge than when you Hygge.

THE ELEMENT OF TOGETHERNESS

When Hygge becomes a social endeavor, it is best enjoyed with friends. Hygge settings are about gatherings, yes, but never about wowing or impressing the guests. There is a fair bit of indulgence when you get together with your loved ones, but never any extravagance.

The element of togetherness does not mean that the company has to be big in numbers. If anything, it can be just one or maybe two to three people from one's close circle of family and friends to Hygge together. A survey showed that 60% of Danes consider three or four people to be the ideal number to Hygge with.

Hygge gatherings have no place for social anxiety or any pressure to present a certain picture of yourself. It gives you the ideal opportunity to take a break from the active outward-focused life. It's only considered Hyggeligt when people gather on common ground to share the vicissitudes of life. The company gathered is sure that no one will challenge them on their opinions and that their difficulties will most likely resemble those of the others present there.

TURN OFF THE TECHNOLOGY

In its true sense, technology doesn't have much of a place in a Hygge lifestyle. That is not to say that you turn every device off in your life, but it does suggest that you put these away when you want to relax.

That is fairly contrary to the accepted norm of relaxing where everyone has a device in their hands, even when at a gathering. People are so engrossed in their own phones or laptops that no one bothers to talk with anyone else. This is not what Hygge is about.

Turning off technology also lets you be present in the moment. Once present, you can then appreciate your time with others, laugh, joke and be merry, and enjoy the company. Hygge gatherings lend an opportunity for people to meet up where they sit down, talk to and listen to each other. If anything, Hygge serves as the antithesis of contemporary etiquette where people are always connected through technology instead of interpersonal experiences.

This digital detox makes you more aware of what's happening in the here and now, where you learn to appreciate what's in front of you.

TURN OFF THE GOSSIP

Many people, consciously or unconsciously, indulge in gossip, rumors, criticism and other negative aspects when together with their friends. Any simple conversation can become an opportunity to complain or speak negatively about someone. This behavior has no place in a Hygge lifestyle. Contrarily, Hygge discourages such negative talk and encourages the positive.

When sitting with your friends and other loved ones, engage in fun and meaningful conversations. As mentioned previously, there is no place for discontent, uneasiness and animosity in Hygge. Talk of anything that engages conflict or ill will in any capacity is prohibited.

PACE YOUR LIFE

An interesting aspect of Hygge is that it lets you slow down the pace of life. Contrary to contemporary practices where most people are on the go 24/7, Hygge involves slowing down to capture a moment.

While many people believe that if they are not busy, then they're either lazy or not determined enough. They set themselves up as not reaching their full potential or even wasting their life away. But slowing down does not make someone a quitter or a failure. Instead, it is a way to practice some self-preservation where you take the time to recover and recharge your body as well as your mind.

Hygge teaches you the importance of slowing down as it involves making time to pause and be gracious. It means taking a deep breath, switching off your gadgets, and listening to what nature has to tell you.

It is a way of taking time to acknowledge the overlooked moments in life. It is also a way to put some perspective and let you see what's important and what's not.

When you learn to do this, you find it easier to enjoy the laughter of children, listen meaningfully to others, and be more aware of your surroundings. As you become aligned with the present moment you feel good and relaxed, your mood becomes optimistic and you enjoy life more.

Slowing down is a practice that makes your life more purposeful while also letting you cultivate patience and gratitude.

Slowing down can be as uncomplicated as taking out ten minutes to meditate every day. It could involve allowing yourself to sit down and catch up on a good read all evening rather than catch up on your to-do list. Or it could be making time to play with your kids and open up space in your life for other people.

BE MINDFUL

When you pace your life, you learn to be more mindful. Some people look at Hygge as a mindfulness practice which lets you enjoy everything you do such as take an extra few minutes to soak in a warm bath, savor the chai latte you just made and carefully monitor the growth of your indoor plants.

By itself, mindfulness teaches you to be present in the moment, which is also the essence of Hygge. It makes you aware of where you are and what you're doing, once again, all important aspects of Hygge. With mindfulness you learn to enjoy the act of brushing your teeth, eating dinner, talking with friends and even exercising.

It's a practice that supports many attitudes that contribute to a satisfying life. It increases your capacity to enjoy experiences as they happen and become fully engaged in the moment. At the same time, mindfulness can also help prepare you better to deal with adverse events.

You can practice mindfulness in several ways, such as mindful journaling. This is a practice where you record all the good things that happen in a day. Journaling will let you frame your day and end it on a positive note. You can also be mindful of the way you eat, as I have mentioned previously, by savoring your food, and enjoying the different textures. Plus, you can also be mindful of the way you spend your money.

Remember that Hygge is not about getting grand and fancy things but keeping things simple? This is where you get to Hygge properly when you can distinguish your wants from your needs and be happy with what you have.

To fully embrace the Hygge lifestyle, you need to embrace its principles in every aspect of your life.

Chapter 11: Signs that You're Deep in Hygge

YOU EXPERIENCE A SENSE OF CALM IN YOUR LIFE

Hygge gives you this sense of peace so you can finally give your mind and body a break. From constantly being on the go, you finally see the importance of slowing down, getting under a soft blanket, giving yourself the space to just breathe.

YOU CAN GO ON FOR DAYS, MAYBE EVEN WEEKS, WITHOUT CONSTANTLY CHECKING YOUR PHONE

From being a total tech and information tech junkie, now you can live a normal life without being a slave to your phone. You use your time for rest to rest, and not mindlessly scroll through your smartphone. You find new ways to connect with your friends without relying too much on the internet.

YOU FEEL THE MOST RELAXED YOU'VE BEEN IN YEARS

Once you get into the habit of taking care of yourself with warm baths, hearty soup, and scented candles, you realize that this is probably the most relaxed you've ever been. Most people are unaware of how stressed they are until they experience the Hygge lifestyle.

YOU HAVE STARTED EATING HEALTHIER

Because Hygge food gives you so much comfort, there's no need to stress eat ever again. Your meals, although simple, are fresh, healthy, and packed with flavor. With Hygge, you finally experience the true meaning behind the saying "have your cake and eat it too".

You spend a lot of your time with family and friends

Instead of spending Saturday night alone wallowing in self-pity, you find that you have more time to be with the people who love you. You enjoy the little moments of connecting with people, whether it's over a cup of tea or sharing a meal. You value emotional connection now more than ever before.

You don't feel guilty about having "me time"

You now understand the importance of taking care of yourself before you can take care of others. You schedule "me time" in your daily routine without having to feel guilty about it ever again.

YOUR CONSTANT HEADACHES AND MIGRAINES HAVE STOPPED

Remember those tension headaches that you used to get before switching to a Hygge lifestyle? They're all gone now, thanks to your regular "me time" sessions and dimmed lighting. Without the bright lights, you can light your favorite candles and finally let go of all the tension you experienced throughout the day.

YOU SLEEP BETTER

Because of your Hygge evening ritual, you find that your sleep quality has drastically improved. You wake up every day well-rested and ready to accept the challenges of a busy day.

YOU HAVE BETTER TIME MANAGEMENT SKILLS

Once you embrace Hygge as a way of life, you don't see the point of rushing through your day. You learn to have a better grasp of time, so you now make it to all your meetings and appointments on time. You also have a better life-work balance now that you've made it a point to finish your tasks on time.

Chapter 12: The Impact of Hygge On Society

To understand how Hygge improves the happiness of an entire society, we must first examine the things that Hygge replaces. We have already mentioned the vicious cycle of consumerism. This endless cycle of addiction will never lead to any lasting sense of happiness. Rather than producing happiness, this hyper-consumerism creates the sense of being unfulfilled. This is because no object can ever bring true happiness and satisfaction.

Only experiences can create that type of joy in a person's life. That is why Hygge is so effective at establishing and maintaining happiness, not only on the individual level but on the social level as well. By focusing on experience rather than possessions, Hygge rescues a person from the endless cycle of consumerism and restores a sense of happiness and contentment that can only be found when a person begins to appreciate the simple pleasures in life. When most individuals in a community share this experience of appreciation, it begins to shape the social dynamic in a very real way. Instead of streets full of people who are stressed out and eager to get their next consumer "fix," you have streets full of people who enjoy day-to-day life and understand and appreciate the things that are truly important in life.

The impact that this economic security has on the individual is obvious, but how does this affect society as a whole? One significant difference between Danish society and American society is the importance placed on work. Since the average Dane has all that they need to live a comfortable, happy and content life, they don't have the raging passion for making more and more money that is so dominant in American culture. This significantly impacts their focus on work. Rather than centering life and activities on work, the people of Denmark center work within their lives. They still have a schedule to work by, and they still have to work well to make their paycheck. However, they don't need to be on standby 24 hours a day, 7 days a week like so many Americans are.

Another way in which Hygge positively impacts society as a whole is that, by eliminating hyper-consumerism, it significantly reduces the waste we create. While consumerist societies can boast of strong production numbers and sales figures, they have to also admit to overwhelming amounts of waste. Some of this waste is the result of more items being produced than are purchased. However, the vast majority of it is the result of perfectly good items being discarded to make room for the latest and greatest 'stuff' available. More and more electronics, clothing, automobiles, and the more are discarded year after year for no other reason than they simply aren't chic enough.

Since Hygge takes the focus off consumerism, the average person living Hygge will use a phone, laptop, and the like until they are no longer functioning. When you multiply this by the number of persons in the society, you reduce overall waste production exponentially. After all, instead of buying a new phone each year, or even worse, every few months, the average Dane will buy a new phone every three to five years or more. The same goes for every other electronic device that they own.

Hygge can have several other positive effects on a society's environment. First and foremost is a reduction in carbon emissions. Since activities such as walking and bicycling are considered very Hygge, the amount of pollution caused by driving cars is significantly reduced in a Hygge society. There's less need to own a car in a place like Denmark. When walking and bicycling are seen as viable alternatives to driving, then even people who do own cars will drive them less and keep the same one longer. This helps to keep the air considerably cleaner. Fewer cars also mean that fewer roads are required, meaning fewer disruptive construction projects. Additionally, fewer cars mean that fewer parking lots are needed, which keeps both the rural and urban landscapes far more visually appealing.

A second way that Hygge helps the environment is that it creates a greater sense of appreciation for one's surroundings. When people take the time to enjoy a walk in the forest, they will be a lot less likely to cut the forest down to build a new Wal-Mart. This is especially true in a society that has turned its collective back on consumerism. Furthermore, when people find happiness and pleasure in their surroundings, they also tend to take better care of those surroundings. Litter, pollution, over-development, and other such harmful acts against nature become things of the past in Hygge societies. Not only does this create an environment that is more harmonious with nature, but one that is healthier for people and all living things.

Nature has been shown to reduce stress and anxiety; therefore, a nature-friendly environment will also be relaxing and calming for anyone living there. Furthermore, the physical health benefits of a nature-friendly environment are highly significant. Better air quality, lower noise pollution, and cleaner water are all abundant in places that protect and appreciate nature. Thus, when a society takes on a Hygge approach to life, the symbiotic relationship between humanity and nature is maintained or restored.

Finally, there is the impact of Hygge on crime and social disorder. While crime will exist in every society to some degree, crime rates are much lower in societies where Hygge is a regular way of life. This is particularly true in the case of violent crime. Studies have shown that stress, anxiety, and the feeling of isolation and being alone are significant factors that contribute to crime in all forms, most especially violent crime.

Chapter 13: Hygge Parenting, Relationships, and Togetherness

One of the most crucial components in practicing Hygge is to encourage and facilitate positive relationships, fostering togetherness. Practicing Hygge can have a profound impact on all your relationships, from parenting with empathy to nurturing a spousal bond to becoming a better friend.

The Hyggelige traditions of communing in cafes and eating family dinners around a set table together create lifelong bonds of affection. Hygge activities also emphasize the importance of spending time with our loved ones with joy and attentiveness. Embracing the simplicity and pleasure of every day is profoundly comforting to all of us - especially children - and recognizing that our highest forms of happiness come from our relationships with others remains at the core of the Hygge way of life.

PARENTS: PARENTING PEACEFULLY

The impact that we have as parents cannot be overstated, and the way that we decide to parent not only affects the physical and psychological health of our children, but it also serves as a model for how our children behave and interact with others out in the world. Eventually, in most cases, this transfers to how your children parent their own kids. The Hygge way of parenting emphasizes togetherness authenticity, and empathy. It may seem, at first glance, that the Hygge lifestyle is for the carefree and childless: afternoons spent lounging in cafes or in front of a fire or reading binges in a cozy and quiet corner. Yet, the underlying values inherent to the concept of Hygge can be applied quite appropriately to parenting styles. Who among us wouldn't embrace the idea of "peaceful parenting?" It may sound easier said than done, but with a few thoughtful tips and techniques, you can incorporate the best of Hygge into your parenting style.

One of the most important parenting techniques you can employ is that of being present with your children. Tune in to their needs and wants, rather than trying to project onto them what you think they might need or want. Get down on their level - literally - and see the world through their eyes

Be sincere and authentic when responding to their interests. Any child of reasonable acuity knows when an adult condescends to them, so respond with genuine questions and support.

Empathy is also a central tenant in Hygge-style parenting (and living, in general); fostering an empathy of others by demonstrating this to your own children creates a bond like no other.

Encourage creative activity: get involved in art projects with your children or play dress-up or make-believe. Nurture their imagination and create a safe space for them to express themselves. Believe it or not, you will gain as much from this interaction as they do.

Encourage play that is stimulating to the senses. While technological devices and computers have a place in our lives, to be sure, there is something to be said for more traditional kinds of tactile play. Consider investing in a sandbox, make models, or play with dough.

Music is also an excellent way to get kids - and yourself - up and moving, while stimulating our bodies and minds. Physical activity is as important to brain development and overall health as is intellectual pursuits.

Always eat together and encourage your children to participate. This ritual cannot be stressed enough! This habit of spending time preparing food, giving thanks, and eating around a table together is a habit for life. Study after study shows the amazing benefits that this one simple ritual can have on children. It makes for more humane, empathetic, and grateful interactions for the rest of their lives.

Playing games together is another key component in fostering a child into adulthood. Games often provide practice for real life - at least in traditional games. With this in mind, try weaning kids away from the phone and the computer, engaging them in other forms of play that help them to model relationships and activities that will assist them in adulthood.

Don't forget to play outside, as well. Nurture a love of the outdoors and empathy for nature, in general. Remember the Danish saying: there is no bad weather, only bad clothing choices.

Read together - another surefire way to create a lifelong, positive habit! Encourage children to spend quiet time reading along, as well. Allow children the space to figure out their own self-care.

Spend some time with physical affection, too. Snuggling and comforting your children is one the most significant things you can do to make them feel safe and happy throughout their lives. When you give them your full attention and engagement, you give them peace and happiness.

Finally, remember to believe in yourself: trusting your Hygge instincts as a parent will give you the confidence, kindness, and patience to nurture your children with love and generosity.

PARTNERS: NURTURING RELATIONSHIPS

We would also do well to consider the foundations of a Hygge lifestyle when approaching our partners, whether they are spouses, significant others, or co-parents. We often forget that relationships take effort, just as raising children to do. Without the same kind of nurturing spirit with which we approach our children, relationships can stagnate or grow untenable. The concept of Hygge is easily applicable to our romantic relationships, and many of the basic tenants of Hygge in and of themselves will foster a healthy connection. For example, creating a comforting and cozy home is a first step toward coming home from work into a welcoming environment, the kind of place where a good mood is easy to come by. Other tips and techniques for maintaining happy love relationships are as follows.

Create good energy throughout your house, especially the places that you interact at an intimate level, such as the bedroom. Fill your home with items that have meaning, rather than material objects that simply advertise wealth or success. You can't buy Hygge; instead, you build it via memory-making and attention to the mundane details of the everyday. Family photographs, mementos from vacations, natural found objects decorate your space in such a way that cements togetherness.

But don't forget yourself. One of the foundational elements in creating a Hygge relationship is to embody Hygge ideals yourself. Self-care is necessary to care for anyone else. Also, think of this in terms of your house: it should remind you not only of your present togetherness, but also of your individual self. Losing yourself in a relationship is not a formula for happiness, but rather a recipe for long-term resentments.

Communication, as we all well know, is key to any constructive relationship. Learn to communicate openly, honestly, authentically, and calmly for best results.
Cooperation is also key to any successful relationship, especially if it involves multiple people and objectives: partners raising children together invariably must cooperate on many fronts, but you also must learn to cooperate within the confines of your one interpersonal relationship. This is reliant on open and honest communication and a desire to put togetherness ahead of other goals.

Leave work at work. This is harder to do than it sounds for many, if not most of us. However, if you are to create a relationship with true togetherness that embodies the spirit of Hygge, then you must pay attention to the ways that your working life invades your home life.

Speaking of dinner, that time is sacred, something to be protected and honored. Make it a habit to keep it sacred.

Use music to set the mood: curate your own playlists for different occasions, different seasons to keep you in the spirit of relaxed happiness.

Slowing down, in general, is the rule of thumb when practicing Hygge. Make special time for your significant other daily, no matter how seemingly simple or limited this might be. Hold hands while watching a movie, take a walk after dinner, commit to an hour before bedtime alone without interruption.

Minimize the excess stuff in your lives, whether it is material or emotional. The baggage of all kinds interferes with peace and happiness.

FRIENDS: ESTABLISHING BONDS

Another crucial factor in practicing Hygge is to form and maintain friendship bonds. Besides your family, friends are the most important connections you have in the world, and ideally, friends fulfill needs that family cannot. Talking to a friend about the stresses you have in raising children is quite different than having that same discussion with a co-parent. Having some time away from family is just as healthy and important as spending quality time with them. Friendships are our way of keeping a sense of our own self separate from the needs and desires of family members. And, just as with children and with intimate relationships, friendships must be nurtured and cultivated with warmth and attention to maintain. One of the most striking facts to emerge out of recent sociological research is that social connection is the best predictor of overall happiness. Thus, we need to establish and maintain the bonds we have with our strongest social connections via friendships and other extended relationships.

Make time to spend with friends regularly. It's wonderful if you can establish a standing date and time to meet with friends each week or create a ritual in which friendly interactions take place with spontaneity and ease.

Invest in friendships by welcoming them into your home: host a monthly Sunday brunch, or Saturday game night, or Friday night card game, or wine Wednesdays, or thirsty Thursdays - whatever works best for your crowd. The point is to make the event a recurring one rather than an occasional one; planning and fuss are kept to a minimum, and your house becomes the welcoming, comforting place to be.

Encourage drop-ins. This is not a typically American attitude in our contemporary society, where we often don't even know our neighbors, but this is an ingrained part of Danish life. If your home is Hygge-fied, then you may find that it happens anyway.

Don't worry about throwing big, elaborate parties to bond with friends. Oftentimes, the most intimate bonding happens with just a handful of people, ideally being three to five. Also, this isn't the point of Hyggelige togetherness anyway; the point is to be relaxed, comfortable, and casual wherein great company can be readily enjoyed.

But do always have good food and drinks on hand. This doesn't have to be fancy, to reiterate, but in the spirit of hospitality, honor your friends with generosity and kindness.

Savor the moment: envision time with friends as you would time with family, a time to unplug from devices and to interact with conviviality and conversation.

Remember that friendship is a choice, unlike family, and with those choices comes a dedication to caring for others outside of your immediate family. This kind of thinking has a definite ripple effect, radiating out from family to friends to neighbors to strangers. Fostering mutual respect and empathetic connection among peoples is at the heart of practicing Hygge.

FAMILY: INTERGENERATIONAL TOGETHERNESS

Everything that can be said above about friendship and most of what can be said about our family relationships also applies to extended family. One of the tragedies of modern American life is that we spend more time with technology than ever and less time with our extended families and elders. So much wisdom is to be gained from maintaining relationships and connection with our grandparents, aunts, uncles, mentors, and others. While this is certainly not relegated just to Hygge practice, the relationships that we can foster with extended family members enrich, enlighten, and enliven our lives in innumerable ways.

Chapter 14: Frugal Hygge

It has been stated repeatedly throughout this book that practicing Hygge does not require lavish expenditures. It is not about money; it is about the experience. Indeed, one of the very tenants of Hygge is to avoid waste and enjoy what exists within the realm of your daily life - simplicity, simplicity, simplicity! Beyond this, however, there are ways to think about Hygge as the happiest kind of frugal life you can lead. Anyone can practice Hygge, no matter what their income and certain activities that are inherently Hygge are also inherently budget-friendly.

Check out some money-saving tips for how to Hygge well and within a budget.

What about all those candles? First, don't spend a fortune on them, whatever you do! It's hard to practice Hygge right without them, and you'll inevitably burn through many, especially in winter. Shop the discount section of department stores for good bargains or seek out places where you can buy in bulk.

What is one of the most Hyggelige activities you can do? **Stay at home**. You don't need to seek out entertainment and transportation. Invite friends over for drinks and a movie, no expensive cocktails or Uber required unless those friends are having more than one or two drinks and intend to drive home. One of the core concepts of Hygge is to be cozy, comfortable, and happy inside your home.
Invest in just a few good, sturdy mugs for drinks at home with friends - coffee, cocoa, glogg, mulled wine, cider, and so on are all lovely in a plain old mug.

Homemade is very Hygge, from food to décor to gifts to socks and scarves. Yes, it takes money to garner the supplies, but it is far less expensive to cook a homemade meal for four than it is to buy it! The same is true for decorative items and well-crafted gifts. Besides, a beautiful hand-drawn card is a keepsake, not just another throwaway for the landfill. You can also customize cheaper store-bought items for a personal touch either for your home or as a gift: throw pillows, cushions, blankets can all easily be gussied up with your personal style. Learn to knit (or invest in a cheater kit), as yarn and knitting needles are far less expensive than buying scarves and hats and so on.

Even if you aren't a very crafty person, you can still write a letter or send a thank you note. Gratitude is at the core of the Hygge way of life, as well, and taking time out of your day for thanks is a frugal way to add some goodness to the world.

Remember reading: talk about a frugal Hygge thrill. Check out books from the library or scour used bookshops to buy plenty of fun and interesting reads. Encourage your friends to borrow and exchange books to widen your repertoire, as well. Start a book club and invite members to your warm and cozy house to talk books and sip mulled wine in front of the hearth.

Take stock of what you need rather than what you desire. Hygge is about returning to simple values and simple pleasures, and we all get caught up in the constant striving of consumer culture at times. One of the most frugal activities you can do is to take inventory of what you have and how much of it you use. It won't take long for you to begin to decide what is necessary and what is clutter.

Short of that, seek out used items for your Hygge needs. Thrift stores and online warehouses offer lots of very affordable items, from comfy sweaters to great reads to household goods. For larger items, such as sofas or other furniture, Craigslist is always a solid option. the idea of recycling, of avoiding waste is central to the Hygge philosophy and Scandinavian society in general.

Start a savings account: if you discover that you lack several things that you'd like to have to refine your Hygge lifestyle, or if you're just starting out, then start a Hygge account for those things. Putting aside a bit from each paycheck will allow you to afford pieces little by little. Having a savings account is a pretty good idea, anyway.

Also, remember that you don't have to do everything all at once. Start with one area of your life or home to begin practicing Hygge. If you have a bike, then bike to the park - that's a start. If you want to start having friends over for game nights, then Hygge up your living room - bedrooms and baths and wardrobe can wait. Take it one piece at a time, and remind yourself that Hygge is a mindset, really, not a bunch of material things.

The simple things are often the best things in life, as well. It doesn't cost anything to spend some time snuggling with a loved one or looking through old pictures for a reminiscence costs nothing and means just about everything. Spending time with loved ones is infinitely better than spending money.

Enjoying a Frugal Life Through Hyggelig Practices

Have Fun with the Whole Group by Playing Board Games.

Compared to popular digital forms of entertainment, such as mobile games and streaming apps, board games are considered as more Hyggelig. When you play a game on your phone, regardless of whether it is a social game or not, the time you can spend for a personal interaction with other people will be significantly lessened.

Instead of just facing a screen, board games can be just as fun while keeping things Hygge for you and your companions. Variety would not likely be an issue because there is a wide array of board games available nowadays.

DESIGNATE A TV OR MOVIE NIGHT EVERY WEEK.

Reserve at least one night each week for watching your favorite TV shows, or the movies that have caught your interest. You might be tempted to binge-watch everything, especially in the age of streaming apps, but spacing out your viewings can turn a solitary activity into a fun hangout with your friends.

CREATE A MINI LIBRARY.

Encourage your neighbors to help you form a mini library that will be shared by all. Gather up the books that you have lying around your home and ask the others to the same. Set aside a dedicated space for the books and arrange them in an orderly fashion.

When everything is set up, establish a rule wherein the borrower would have to leave a book whenever they want to borrow one from the library. In this way, you would maintain the number of books while increasing its diversity. You would also get to enjoy new titles without having to buy it on your own.

ATTEND OUTDOOR FILM SCREENINGS.

Outdoor cinemas are quite popular during summertime in several cities. Compared to watching movies in traditional theaters, doing it outside tends to be cheaper, but still fun way to spend time with your loved ones, friends, and family.

To make this a Hyggelig outing, you should make the most of its less formal setting. Spending hours out in an open field and under the stars could be quite relaxing or romantic, depending on who you are with. You can also bring along food and drinks with you so that you can have a mini picnic while watching the movie.

SWAP GIFTS USING CURRENT BELONGINGS THAT ARE NO LONGER IN USE.

Do you have something in your basement that you have stored there for future use, but have never had a reason to bring it out again since then? Or perhaps someone has given you an electric kettle as a gift but you already have one in the first place. Rather than waiting for the occasion where you may find some use for it, why not invite your family and friends for a simple gathering where you can all swap items that you are not using at all?

Such parties can be quite Hyggelig because of all the good spirit and fun times that it could bring for everyone participating in it. You might think that you could just sell the stuff on a garage sale, a flea market, or somewhere on the Internet. However, none of those options can provide you a Hyggelig experience at all.

COMPLETE DIY PROJECTS.

Challenge yourself with DIY projects that you may then use for decorating your home or workstation, or for gifting to your loved ones. In comparison to pre-made ones that are normally sold in shops, DIY items tend to be much, much cheaper. However, take note that you do have to invest your time instead to turn a project into a success.

Aside from nifty little trinkets and artworks, try to create homemade beauty products from scratch. Just make sure to research for a recipe that comes with a guarantee from others, and that you could easily follow.

MAKE SMARTER PURCHASES.

Frugal living does not mean that you have to settle for whatever is the cheapest. Instead, it requires you to be smarter when it comes to evaluating whether or not you should purchase a particular item. Through this, you may be assured that you are getting the best value for your money.

Hygge also promotes quality over quantity in everything that you do. Therefore, instead of buying something that would break after a couple of uses—this prompting you to purchase a replacement—opt for something that could last for a longer period, even with regular use.

Finding, saving, and using coupons for purchases could help you save money, too. Through these, you would either keep yourself from paying the full price or get you an extra item for a lesser price—or sometimes, for free!

Keep in mind though that the usage of coupons, as well as purchasing a discounted item, could only be considered as a sign of frugal living if the item you wish to buy is something that you need or want. If your reason for buying it is mainly due to the supposed savings that you would get from doing so, then what you are doing runs against the principles of Hygge.

LEARN HOW TO REPAIR AND MAINTAIN THINGS THAT YOU FREQUENTLY USE.

Equipping yourself with these kind of skills would help you save a lot of money every year. Since learning how to do major repairs could take a lot of time, you should focus first on figuring out how to troubleshoot and do minor repairs and maintenance works for things like:

- Your car, motorcycle, or bicycle
- The plumbing of your house
- Replacement of batteries for smoke detectors
- Sanding and repainting of walls or cabinets
- Installing different types of locks on doors

Frugal living based on Hyggelig principles is not about depriving yourself. Instead, it is about becoming more resourceful so that you may still enjoy your favorite things in life without having to spend so much money for it. It about finding out creative ways to save money so that you could truly enjoy your days once you have retired from work, or so that you could achieve your dream of traveling the world one day.

Chapter 15: Improving Work Performance and Satisfaction Through Hygge

The practice of Hygge goes beyond the home and yourself. It can also be used to enhance the working environment to promote collaboration, productivity, and wellbeing of the employees.

How is this possible?

When work satisfaction is high, it creates an atmosphere that is conducive for the achievement of the following:

THE WELLBEING OF THE EMPLOYEES

Several organizations that are considered as leaders of their respective fields recognize the value of ensuring the wellbeing of their employees. Aside from preventing them from being overly fatigued and vulnerable to sickness, the improvement of employees' wellbeing contributes to their ability to produce more creative and innovative output. Furthermore, studies show that placing a high value on wellbeing enables the organization to retain its employees for a longer period, and dissuades them from thinking of leaving the organization for a competitor.

Given these benefits, many businesses nowadays seek for ways to understand how they could foster the wellbeing of their respective employees. Experts point them to various strategies, one of which is the concept of Hygge.

How exactly does a Hyggelig workspace enhance the wellbeing of employees?

PHYSICAL WELLBEING

Experts in workspace design recommend the provision for seats and desks that allows various types of posture. Requiring the employees to just sit down while they work can be particularly detrimental to their health. As such, the workplace must include furniture that may be used while standing up or lounging about as well.

COGNITIVE WELLBEING

Hygge wants you to form a strong connection with nature, but it can be hard to do so when you have to work for most of the day. Some organizations provide their employees with this opportunity by taking inspiration from nature for their interior decoration.

This does not mean having to spend thousands of dollars just to turn the office green. One of the simplest and most Hyggelig ways to do so is by setting up parts of the workplace dedicated to live plants. Depending on the level of commitment and the available space that may be allocated for it, this may be done by creating a mini garden somewhere in the premises, or by arranging potted plants around the office.

EMOTIONAL WELLBEING

Aside from assuring the physical and mental wellbeing of the employees, it is also important and beneficial, in the long run, to care for their emotional stability. Through this, they would be able to feel more at ease with their superiors, teammates, and subordinates.

Some employees feel obliged to eat their lunch in their workstations so that they can stay on top to catch important emails as they arrive, or so that they can make plans for their next projects. Having this kind of habit can be abrasive not only to your cognitive performance but also for your emotional wellbeing.

COLLABORATION AMONG THE EMPLOYEES

Hygge supports the collaboration of employees by promoting activities and set-ups that encourages openness, kindness, and communication. Traditional means of achieving this, like conducting daily briefings and assigning the employees into group projects, could only work to some level. Bringing them closer to one another on a much deeper level requires the application of Hyggelig principles on the day to day operations of the business.

Embracing the spirit of teamwork is an integral step in achieving a Hyggelig workspace. As such, employers should give importance to exercises that enhance the sense of belongingness of the employees among each other.

Teambuilding activities take time to plan and execute, however. To give you a head-start on this, here are some excellent ideas that are aligned with the principles of Hygge:

Hygge has originally been developed by the Danish people to combat the harsh conditions they experience during wintertime. Nowadays, it is no longer just limited to cold, dark nights. Its scope continues to widen as people continually discover ways of introducing Hygge to different aspects of life, including the workplace.

Happiness, comfort, and security may not be the first things you think of when asked about the best ways to increase the productivity and creativity of the employees. However, as exhibited by the Danes and the various studies conducted about the effects of working in a Hyggelig workplace, it has been proven that bringing in the comforts and familiarity of a home to the workplace ensures the overall wellness of the employees and enhances the way they collaborate. These two points contribute significantly to the employee's work satisfaction—which is considered as one of the key factors that bring the performance and profitability of the company to even greater heights.

Chapter 16: Daily Habits to Assist You to Get Out of Your Mind

How we approach our job is greatly determined by our disposition. If we are in a mentally strong place, this is effortless. If we are depressed or stressed, everything seems exhausting. As important as it is to be good at everything you do it's equally important to practice your own strategy and learn who you are.

Here are 5 methods to nurture a favorable mindset:

MAKE TIME FOR 'INPUT MODE'

If you are always in "output" mode, you will eventually run dry. 'Output' style is when you are calling on yourself to make, create or 'do' – essentially, to put something out into the world.

Input mode, on the other hand, is whenever you're replenishing yourself, your knowledge lender, your motivation or your own psychological condition. For example, reading is an input signal. Watching a good movie is an input signal. Meditation is a particularly strong input signal, and sleep is perhaps the most important one.

SURROUND YOURSELF WITH POSITIVE PEOPLE

You are the sum of the individuals with whom you spend the most time.

Look around. If you are surrounded by clever people, they will raise your standards and you'll wind up smarter than you were before. Conversely, if you are surrounded by less intelligent men and women, then this may become your normal mindset and you'll follow similar patterns.

EXERCISE

Confidence is the result of not only doing something but understanding that you do that thing well. When you exercise frequently, you become better at it. If you are good, you are feeling confident about your skills, and if you are feeling confident about your skills, you take more risks, try harder, and finally become a master of your craft.

Likewise, if you do not exercise, you will not feel as good about your abilities. Therefore, you will not take as many risks, you will become insecure, and you won't exercise often. This means you take hardly any significant strides on your path to greatness.

FIND ROLE MODELS

In the end, the secret to fostering an optimistic mindset is to find somebody who you admire who will teach you how they have done it.

There is no quicker and much more effective method to find out in life than to locate a mentor. Simply being in the presence of somebody who has learned how to use their particular mindset to its optimum ability, you will start to pick up their strategy.

The reason that this is so crucial is that a role model is somebody who has gone through their own journey. They've overcome challenges and discovered their very own secrets and techniques permitting them to create their very own distinct strategy for living their best lives. By analyzing someone who operates in this manner, you may learn what it is which enables them to be this effective, simultaneously moving through your own process of discovery - except at a far greater speed.

GET SOME SUNSHINE

Sunlight and exercise often go together. This depends on what part of the world you reside in; just how much sun can be found during the season as well as how realistic it is that to devote some of your time to the outdoors.

Obtaining too little sun is bad for your mind. Higher quantities of vitamin D in your system permit you to perform better and may also slow down the aging of your own mind. However, too much sun can be very harmful to your skin, promoting skin cancer and sunburns. You always have the option to take vitamin D supplements should you discover that you are not capable of getting out of the house as much as you'd like.

BUILD POWERFUL CONNECTIONS

If you feel lonely, it can lead to emotional and cognitive decline, since these feelings have a negative influence on your sleep, increase your blood pressure, and can lead to depression a general decrease in wellbeing.

Most entrepreneurs understand how to build and maintain relationships. The important thing is to create a solid support system for yourself, as that will allow you to remain healthy emotionally over a long period.

MEDITATE

Meditation is a trending subject amongst several entrepreneurs today, and its advantages are difficult to dispute. Meditation is primarily known for lowering stress levels and it may additionally prevent gastrointestinal disorders like Alzheimer's or dementia.

SLEEP WELL

This can be another tricky problem for entrepreneurs. Frequent early mornings and late nights along with the anxieties or delight involved in building and developing a company can have undesirable side effects on sleep routines.

Sleep is needed to combine learning and memory. If you do not receive enough sleep, then the grey matter at your frontal lobe can start to degenerate. Your frontal lobe controls and supports your working memory in addition to performance, which makes it very important.

EAT WELL

It should not come as a surprise that nutrition plays a crucial role in your mental health. Entrepreneurs tend to be rushing from one meeting to another, which gives them very little, if any, opportunity to eat well.

You need to concentrate on getting the perfect balance of nourishment. Vitamins and amino acids are especially important, and lots of vitamin E is also advantageous. Nuts, whole grains, and avocados can also be favorable for your health, both mental and physical. What is good for your body tends to be even better for your mind.

MASTER YOUR MINDSET

If you have ever neglected to reach any goals in your life, the issue could be with your mind. That is how significant your mindset is to your life. Your brain is the strongest force.

The stories you educate yourself with and the things you think about yourself may prevent change from occurring or new ideas from blossoming.

When you start to acknowledge your mindset, you'll be able to make fresh, healthy decisions, adopt a positive outlook in life, dedicate yourself to your objectives and get them done.

You will likely finish what you start and begin leading the wonderful life you crave and expect. It is within your reach if it's possible to devote time to your goals and dreams.

MAKE SMALL CHANGES

The quest to be a better version of yourself frequently seems just like a roller coaster. It is hard, and it is usually very irregular.

However, life is a journey, not a marathon, and that means that you constantly have another chance to restart and improve. Be patient with yourself. Self-growth is tender; it is sacred ground. There is no better price.

When you're searching for change, so you need to begin adopting change in tiny ways. If you would like to modify your own 'life' rather than be 'ordinary' then you've got to do something different.

MAKE YOUR MORNINGS EASIER

Give yourself 20 minutes every night to make your mornings easier. Plan your own to-do list for the next day before the night ends. Prepare coffee and pick your own clothes.

Your evening ritual decides how productive the next day will be for you. Everything you do just before going to bed involves a great deal to do with all the time you'll be able to awaken with no struggle.

Chapter 17: Experiencing Hygge All Year Long

PRACTICING HYGGE DURING SPRINGTIME

Extreme cold is not a prerequisite for the practice of Hygge. Springtime could be still Hyggelig when you slow down and celebrate the return of the warmer months with your family and friends.

To do so, here are some great ideas that you should try doing once the long winter nights have ended:

JOIN OR CREATE YOUR OWN COMMUNITY GARDEN.

Doing this activity would inspire an uptrend in Hygge on a bigger scale. Nowadays, you can find at least one community garden per town or city. If there is none near you, then you can ask permission from the local government to start one. It is also advisable to get other people on board this early on, so you could get their help with the plans and initial funding for the project.

There are plenty of benefits that could make this initiative worth your while. Studies show that taking care of plants can be relaxing for the body and mind. Since you will do it with other people, you would also be able to connect with other people and nature. As such, it can be both meditative and Hyggelig for everyone participating in it.

GO CYCLING.

Aside from candles and Lego, the Danes are widely known for their love of cycling. They use their bikes when they go to work, to school, or for running errands. Recreational cycling, especially in summer, is arguably the most Hyggelig of these, however.

Using a bicycle for whatever purpose lets you enjoy the sun and breeze as you speed along the streets. It gets the blood pumping without overly exhausting you in the process. It does not emit gases that are harmful for both the body and the environment. Ultimately, cycling makes people feel happier and healthier.

PRACTICE DRAWING OR PAINTING OUTDOOR SCENES.

During springtime, trees and flowers begin to regain their vibrancy and beauty after a long cold season. Simply watching this happen can be a Hyggelig experience, but it would be a lot more rewarding if you would capture this in a drawing or a painting.

Remember to invite your family and friends, too. Prepare a nice picnic with cheeses, fresh fruit, and wine to turn this into a cultured but relaxing experience.

HYGGE LIVING DURING SUMMER

Though summer is not exactly the season for candles and hot chocolate, it can be filled with Hygge, too.

For many, summer means tanned skin, swimming, and lots of sunscreen. It can also mean warm nights spent by grilling barbecue and drinking beer with your family and friends.

The kind of activities that you plan for summer might be totally different compared to those you want to do during winter, but that does not mean that those activities will be devoid of Hygge. As long as you are doing things that make you feel warm, comfortable, and connection with other people and nature, then you would be experiencing a Hyggelig summer.

For your guidance, here are the top 5 recommended activities that you should try doing next summer:

PICK FRUITS AT AN ORCHARD.

Spending the day at an orchard to pick fruits from the trees is extremely Hyggelig. You can choose any kind of orchard, but in Denmark, apple orchards are the most popular ones. Once you have gathered enough fruits, you may block off your schedule for the following day to turn the fresh fruits into jams or sweet preserves. Others also make use of certain fruits for making special cider.

Invite your family and friends for a barbecue.

Grilling meat and sausages over an open fire is one of the widely practiced Hyggelig activity across the world. Barbecue has a universal quality, wherein almost every culture has its own version of it.

To make it more pleasant, throw a barbecue party with the people you care about. Make sure to get a nice variety of meat and vegetables for everyone's enjoyment.

Have a picnic by the beach.

The beach is not just for swimming or sunbathing. It can also be a great site for a picnic with your loved ones.

Summer ushers in the peak season for farmers' markets. As such, you may be able to get a nice selection of fresh fruits, cheeses, and breads for a bountiful picnic. Make it even more Hyggelig by preparing a thick, fluffy blanket where you and your companions can lay into while chatting, eating, and relaxing at the beach.

Welcoming Autumn the Hygge Way

During the Fall, the temperature starts dropping once more until it finally gives way to another winter season. You might think that this would dampen everyone's spirit, but as you may have observed, Autumn is one of the more festive seasons for many people.

Those who practice Hygge would likely agree with this. As the nights starts to grow longer and colder, they also begin to spend more time indoors, cuddling and relaxing by the fire together with family and friends. To make this season extra Hyggelig, here are some top recommendations for you:

BAKE SPECIAL TREATS FOR YOUR FAMILY AND FRIENDS.

Freshly baked goods, such as cakes, cookies, and breads, can be made extra special if you would personally bake them for yourself and for your loved ones.

The act of baking itself tends to be therapeutic. Kneading a dough, and watching it rise could be quite satisfying, even without having to taste yet the results of your hard work.

Serve these baked treats when you have invited over some company, or wrap them up nicely so that you can give them as gifts for the people you care about.

GO TO A SAUNA.

A sauna, or also known as sudatory, is a place where you can relax your body and mind through controlled heat sessions. The Danes, in particular, are known for having a weekly trip to the sauna so that they can unwind and recharge themselves.

Going to a sauna during autumn is extremely Hyggelig, especially when you also use your time there to reflect about the people, things, and experiences that you feel grateful for. Remember to keep yourself hydrated though, especially when you plan to stay long inside the sauna.

CAPTURE AUTUMNAL SCENES THROUGH PICTURES.

In countries that experience the full colors of fall, foliage tours are quite popular activities for the locals and tourists alike. This activity involves exploring areas, typically forests and mountains, where the leaves are beginning or have already changed colors.

During a foliage tour, take the time to look for the most beautiful spots that you would want to capture through a camera. Aside from preserving the memory, these pictures could serve as your way of bringing in a part of nature into your home or workplace. Frame the photos that you have taken and display them somewhere that you could see whenever you feel tired or stressed out. The golden colors of autumn, along with the memories of your experience back then, could help soothe your body, mind, and spirit.

Based on these suggestions, you can easily practice and experience Hygge all year round. You are not limited to these examples though. As long as you can turn something into a joyful, warm, or cozy occasion, then it would be considered a Hyggelig activity.

Another important thing to keep in mind is to keep things simple as much as you can. You do not have to spend a lot of money to practice Hygge through the different seasons of the year. Turn your focus on your feelings from doing a particular activity rather than the opinions of other people about you.

Chapter 18: Adding Hygge into Your Life with These Inexpensive Tricks

The good news is that you can make your home more Hyggelig without having to spend a lot of money in the process. Some of the methods that you can use include:

ADD IN SOME REPURPOSED WOOD

Wood is considered one of the most inviting of the textures because it can add in some more warmth to the home, something that a lot of other textures are just not able to do.

Sometimes, you are lucky enough to just be able to take the carpet out of your home and you will find some nice hardwood floors there, but since this is not likely for most homes, you may need to find other things.

ADD IN SOME OF YOUR MEMORIES

You can leave these pictures out wherever you would like them. They work well on a mantelpiece or on one of your end tables. If you have a wall that is pretty blank and you would like to make it look a bit nicer, you could do a collage of these pictures and help to add to the hominess of the area. In some cases, you may have a larger wall to take care of, and adding in some of your favorite artwork can help to fill this up. Get creative and make that area look like it is important, rather than just ignoring it.

MAKE YOUR OWN BLANKETS

If you want to add in some more of the coziness to the whole home and you don't want to spend a lot of money on blankets, then, make some of your own. This could fit back in with the hobby category that we were talking about earlier, in that you will be able to spend some of your time working on the projects and then you can use them to make your home match up with Hygge as well. If you aren't good at knitting or crocheting, find someone who will be able to help you get this done or ask others if they could give you gifts of blankets for some of the major holidays.

ADD THE ANTIQUES

This may sound a bit like we are trying to make things more expensive, but you can score some great deals if you are looking around. First, see if any family members are trying to get rid of a few of the antiques that they own, ones that are gathering up dust in their homes but that you would be able to add into your home and give them a new work. In addition, you could go to some auctions or garage sales where these antiques have been lying around for a long time and you can pick them up for just a few dollars, decorating your home and making it look amazing without having to spend too much.

WORK ON THE STORAGE

One thing that we haven't talked about much in this guidebook, but which is very important to the idea of

Hygge is that organization is important. It is not a good idea to keep a lot of stuff that you don't need; because messiness and hoarding are not ideas of Hygge. Now you won't be able to get rid of everything in your home, but you do need to make sure that each thing has its own place so that it can be kept away from others and not out in the way all the time.

Setting up for Hygge in your life doesn't have to be difficult. one of the main proponents of Hygge is to keep things simple and easy. This is why it is possible to use some of these simple ideas and inexpensive items to help you to get some more Hygge into your life. Try a few of them out to get some of the Hygge that you would like and to help you to relax and feel good in your own home.

Conclusion

When it comes to defining, categorizing, and identifying Hygge, the term "lifestyle" does not quite capture it. With many lifestyles, there are certain rules, strategies, practices, and mantras. Hygge, however, does not encompass rules, regulations, products, or even stereotypical mantras. It encompasses a **feeling**. It's easy: you simply promote the idea of self-awareness.

Being self-aware in the lifestyle of Hygge is essential, especially for those who have been raised in a culture where emotion is something to cast off to the side in favor of other things. For those raised in cultures where emotion and feelings are even considered one's downfall, the lifestyle of Hygge can be almost impossible to understand, much less promote. But to people in these types of cultures, Hygge can be the most freeing and healthy lifestyle they can choose to live.

Hygge is not merely the promotion of relaxation and comfort, though that is how one gauges whether or not Hygge is being achieved. Promoting these aspects of life enable inward health, from physical healing to mental rejuvenation. The reduction of stresses and anxieties help the body heal from the damage that stress induces over long periods. The reduction of stress reduces levels of damaging chemicals, which can elicit everything from life-threatening fatigue to chronic, debilitating migraines. Allowing the body to relax enables organs to filter the cortisol from your bloodstream and muscle tissue so that automatic immune responses can kick into overdrive and begin to repair the body.

Hygge lives by one guideline and one guideline alone: "Treat yourself with kindness." In a world where people are constantly distracted with things that seem more important than their overall health, it is hard to convey the importance of recognizing that you are the only one responsible for taking care of you.

PART II: LAGOM

Introduction

We have all heard of Hygge the Danish concept of comfort, but how many of us are aware of the Swedish concept of Lagom? Few of us that's for sure, but Lagom is about to be the next big lifestyle choice for many of us feeling trapped by excessive consumerism and waste.

Let's face it we lead very wasteful lives; we throw food away at a tremendous rate. Even our relationships have become wasteful and ever easier to move on to the next one without having to put the work in that previous generations did.

In this book we will look at how we can use the concept of "the right amount is best" to make our lives easier and less wasteful. We will look at how we can apply Lagom to all the important aspects of our lives from our homes to our relationships and lots more in-between.

So slip out of your Danish Hygge for a brief period and embrace living with "Just Enough" Swedish style!

The following chapters will discuss the Swedish secret to happy and fulfilling lives. It may go against a lot of what we value and are used to in our American culture, but with so many people searching for something more, something that will help to bring about more happiness, it could be just what you are looking for.

In this guidebook, we will spend some time looking at the Swedish lifestyle of Lagom (pronounced "lah-gome"). This is a word that means "just enough". You do not want to have too much of something, but you do not want to go so much to the extreme that you will not be able to enjoy life either. With Lagom, there are no extremes, we get just enough of everything that we want or need, and this leads to a happier and healthier life than ever before.

When you are ready to learn more about the Swedish philosophy of Lagom, and you are ready to simplify your life to add in more happiness, make sure to continue reading this guidebook and learn more about how to get started.

Chapter 1: What is Lagom and How Do I Start?

Lagom, pronounced Lar-gohm, is a Swedish word that translates to 'just the right amount'. In a less literal sense, Lagom refers to a lifestyle which strives for a balance between work and rest, expense and frugality. It's a national core value that can make people happier and more productive. And that is probably enough for some to try it. We know that Lagom is a Swedish word. If we consult our lexicons, a standard literal translation from Swedish to

English will use the following words to define the word Lagom:

Just right

Adequate

Sufficient

Enough

Those words give us hints as to the other nuances that are related to it. Because of the implications of such terms we can say that maybe that is the reason why a lot of times the word Lagom is translated as:

Suitable

In balance

In moderation

In other words, simply put, when we say Lagom we are referring to something that is just the right amount. It will carry that peculiar connotation of appropriateness. However, do take note that it does not demand perfection. You don't have to be perfect to be Lagom. Flawlessness isn't part of the gradations of its meaning. What you're looking for is a balance, but you don't have to be perfectly balanced to be truly Lagom.

People who embrace the Lagom lifestyle seek a middle ground of owning just enough, but not too much and working hard enough for life to be fulfilling, but not to the extent that life is stressful. Lagom also involves finding the correct mental balance and peace; a balancing act between enjoying life but also working hard and managing responsibilities.

Lagom is also associated with the concept of fairness, sharing, and equality. In its most basic form, it is thought that sharing what you have will make you happier. This is not only because giving to others makes us happy, but it also encourages others to give to us in return – everyone benefits.

Naturally, Lagom also involves concepts of environmental sustainability and ecological awareness. Fundamental concepts such as not living beyond your means and sharing are applied to nature itself, encouraging society to take care of the planet and avoid needless waste or damage. As the world becomes more globalized, societies in the West have demonstrated a growing concern in the philosophies and lifestyles of other cultures. Lagom offers an alternative to the exotic and grossly misinterpreted ideas from the East; instead of advocating a simple, secular and straightforward approach to happiness and health.

The lifestyle changes associated with Lagom are changes you've probably already considered or at least been recommended.

They include recycling more, saving energy, wasting less water, eating healthily, ensuring you always eat breakfast and so on. Whilst each of these changes might not produce a large effect on their own, together they can start to create a rich and easy-going lifestyle which benefits not only you but also everyone else too.

To start, we need to explore the ideas behind minimalism. Minimalism - which is the art of having less - is a big trend that has made its way into many different aspects of our lives including our home, our work, food, apparel, and so much more. We find that we may meal prep with fewer and more basic ingredients because it saves time and money. We learn how to cut down what is in our wardrobes to help make decisions easier and to reduce the footprint we are leaving on the planet. We stop buying as much stuff that we do not need so that our homes will not feel as cluttered in the long run.

While most of us understand what minimalism, all is about and how it is meant to work. While consuming less will make us feel less debt to an item, we also need to explore more about this topic. Especially, we need to look at what minimalism means to other people, or what Lagom means to other countries.

This brings us to our discussion of Lagom. Lagom is the Swedish art of balanced living. We can translate this word to being "not too little, not too much, just right." This may sound confusing, but it is a good way to help us stay busy and not become lazy, without having to take on too much in our work life, our home lives, and in all of the other aspects that surround us daily.

As someone who is already a minimalist (or is at least thinking about becoming a minimalist), it is important to always do an evaluation of what is around you to see how much you can live without and still be comfortable, and even see what you can live without or how to live with less. The question here is: what if the issue we are facing is not continuing to eliminate or hoard? What it is more about finding the equilibrium that is perfect for our lifestyles without having to cause a lack or an excess in the process? The idea behind Lagom is not that you want to try to reach perfection. Instead, it is all about finding a simple and attainable kind of solution to the daily worries that you go through. This could include things like making sure you have enough downtime, eating better, reducing the amount of stress that you have, and even achieving more happiness. It will help us to learn how to balance work and life so that we can sustain it all and have them all exist harmoniously with one another.

The thing to remember when you are working with Lagom is that our days will shift and sometimes, no matter how hard we try, we are not able to fit it in everywhere. This is part of the beauty of living Lagom: if you cannot check everything off the list each day, that is not a big deal. Just keep the fuss out of the whole situation and make your day as fulfilling and relaxing as you can.

With Lagom, you need to make sure that your aim is to have a fuss-free lifestyle. This means that we need to learn how to find contentment and pleasure in the things that we already have, even if what we have is not picture-perfect. Also, make your goal to understand how all the things that we do play an important part in how we will live a life that is less destructive, and more sustainable, on this earth.

Not everyone who decides to embrace the idea of Lagom wants to be able to adopt it daily, doing it all of the time. It is easy to admit that going with a lifestyle that is free of all the stress and fuss probably sounds pretty ideal. In a culture where over-indulgence is the norm and you are looked down on if you are not able to keep up with what the neighbors have, it is nice to think that there are many other methods that you can rely on. Lagom shows you how to sit back and relax, live with less stuff, and enjoy the life that you are living now.

When you first hear about this term, you may assume that it is the same as the popular "hygge" that was available a few years ago. It was almost impossible to head out anywhere or even enter a bookstore without seeing a lot of information on the Norwegian and Danish word that meant coziness. There will be some similarities occurring between two ideas; hopefully you will be able to see through this guidebook that the Lagom ideology is a bit different.

While this term will seem similar, there are some key differences. First off, hygge is about coziness and being comfortable, and Lagom is more about "just the right amount." The basic idea that comes with this lifestyle philosophy is that we need to find a good harmonious balance and the right amount of happiness. The goal is not having too much, but also not having too little in your life. We will also spend some time looking at the history that comes with Lagom. The Swedes believe that the best way for anyone to live a happy life, they must follow the precepts of Lagom. You deprive yourself of nothing, but you also make sure that you are not overdoing things. Moderation is the key here, and it is the best way for you to create a life that is balanced and fulfilling.

This idea is so indoctrinated into the culture of Sweden that it is visible in all of the different aspects of their life, from their work-life to their homes, and you can even find this idea in their political system. Everyone in this culture should have enough, but not too much – that is the essential principle that the people of Sweden stick with, and it ends up working great for them and their happiness levels.

Lagom is unique in that it strikes a nice balance between hygge and minimalism. You do not need to be heated up by piles of cozy blankets or burn the house down with all your scented candles! Likewise, you do not need to feel like you can only own one spoon, throwing out all the other things that you own. This is where Lagom is the best option because it allows you to meet in the middle between these two lifestyle ideas.

This is a kind of lifestyle that works so well because it will help leak over into all of the areas of your life, and not just one or two. Having a good work and life balance, having just the right number of possessions, being able to reduce the amount of stress that you have, and keeping a healthy amount of frugality are all essential. It can even go all the way down to eating the right amount of food at mealtimes and choosing the right clothes.

With some of these ideas in mind, it is now time for us to learn a few of the simple methods that you can use to help improve your life and ensure that you will use the ideas of Lagom a bit better. Some of the ways that you can work on adding some more Lagom in your life will include the following:

ORIGINS OF LAGOM

Although usually translated as 'in moderation', the word Lagom has no direct equivalent in English. In general, many Swedish words contain denser, richer meanings than their English equivalents and it can be quite hard to translate the subtle nuances and unique flavors of the language.

Several countries have words with a similar meaning, but for the Swedes, the word Lagom carries a special importance – it is a concept to live your life by.

According to myth, the word Lagom originates from historic Viking practices. When drinking together, people in Viking society would drink from the same horn or bowl.

To ensure that everyone gets a good swig, the concept of 'laget om', a fair portion, developed.

Laget om can also be understood as 'enough to go around', evoking the concept of sharing and social responsibility that is also found within the modern concept of Lagom. Over time, laget om supposedly evolved into Lagom and the notion of moderation in all things.

Etymologists reasonably disagree with the Viking story. More realistically, the word Lagom is derived from the root word 'laghum' which means 'according to law'. Whilst living according to the law is undoubtedly part of Lagom, the idea of Lagom has become so much more.

Although it can be considered a lifestyle or a principle, Lagom can be used in general conversation. When a Swedish person asks how you are, *Lagom* is an appropriate answer, similar in feeling to 'great', 'just right' or 'perfect'.

Lagom can also be used to describe the weather, or when something hits the right spot (such as describing a good meal).

Similarly, as with everything in life, the ideal equalization is to be found in the center, and there are numerous exercises that we can gain from the Swedish idea of Lagom and apply to our own lives.

Lagom enables us to expel ourselves from the limits, to discover balance in the center. Boundaries can often be imped our physical and passionate health. We gorge and enjoy, at that point end up attempting to adhere to a carefully characterized system of food to redress. When we're done, we're back to overindulging. At the office, we put in since quite a while ago, focused on hours, never happy with our work, always endeavoring to be "the best." We carry our work home with us, browsing our email in the middle of making supper and putting the children to bed. We are left occupied, depleted, and feeling a long way from fruitful. We have an inclination that we don't have any command over our lives as we're endeavoring to do such a large number of things yet do none of them well.

In the present current culture of style and structure magazines, VIPs, and web-based social networking, we're always immersed with what we figure we "should" be. "I should work out additional. I ought to mingle more. I ought to get more sleep. I ought to eat better. I ought to have superior activity. I should cook more. I ought to become familiar with another dialect. I ought to travel.

What we should gain from the possibility of Lagom is that we enable ourselves to be 'simple enough.'

Rather than utilizing these driving forces to provoke us to create as individuals, they become obstructions, and rather than motivation, motivations to chide ourselves. They frustrate as opposed to giving consolation. They drive us towards a social challenge that leaves us depleted. We aren't happy with what we have and what our identity is. We are rather continually in the interest of additional. "If no one but I can get to the subsequent stage, at that point I'll be happy." This individual and futile social way of life get difficult to get away, and once on this track we're just centered around that following stage, which we think will prompt happiness, harmony, and satisfaction. In any case, these are things that must be found in the present, in that space where we are living in offset with ourselves and our general surroundings.

It is wrong to accept that Lagom implies keeping down, that if we can discover fulfillment with what our identity is and where we are in life, we will get static. As people, we are continually adapting, continually creating. Lagom doesn't mean putting the entirety of that on hold, however it implies discovering happiness in our very own development as people, any place that advancement leads. If we don't wind up getting famous inside our field, or if we don't wind up making a six-figure compensation, that is OK. What our identity is isn't characterized by our triumphs or our disappointments, we are characterized by how we live with them.

Lagom's advantages are not restricted to individual ones. In this cutting-edge world where we live hugely, our impression has incurred significant damage. We have greater houses and greater vehicles. We purchase more and, thus, discard more. We lead lives of overabundance and waste. At the point when we are progressively moderate about our decisions, we decrease our effect. Applying elements of Lagom to our regular daily existences can make us feel much improved, yet in addition help us to seek after a progressively manageable way, since when we are happy with the perfect measure of all things, we live in better offset with ourselves, our locale, and our condition. Live Lagom is a test for you to consider moderate living. Similarly, that the Slow Food development has carried more attention to what we eat, where it originates from, and how we set it up, a moderate life is a deliberate life, one that doesn't take excessively or cause any mischief, and one that spotlights on the basic.

LET CURIOSITY TAKE YOU BY THE HAND

Curiosity is the first step before you can apply the Lagom lifestyle. Be curious and not judgmental. Discover areas in your life where you can apply the facets of this type of living. You don't have to apply its principles to every aspect of your life.

You can do it one step at a time one part of your life at a time. Remember the simple Goldilocks principle: not too much, not too little, but just right. Let's look at several areas where we can apply this peculiar Nordic lifestyle choice.

Your Stuff

I think you can agree that in our modern society a lot of us are preoccupied with accumulating stuff—lots of stuff. Just check out how many clothes you have in your closet. How many toys does your kid have? How many shoes do you have in the house?

Now, how about your kitchen? Find out how many gizmos you have in there. Do you have more than one blender, coffee maker, knives, kitchen tools, juicers, and others? Do you need all of that stuff?

Remember that Lagom is all about embracing sustainability as one's way of life. As it was already pointed out it entails not consuming too much. That also means you have to make choices that are ultimately environment-friendly.

You can ask yourself the following questions:

- Which part of the house do I have too much stuff?

- Which rooms in my home are overstuffed?

- Do you I have two or three things that serve the same function?

- Do I have a lot of single-use items that I just throw away later?

- Do I have hand me downs or do I give away hand me downs?

Chapter 2: The Benefits of Lagom and Why You Should Pursue It NOW!

YOU CAN TAKE YOURSELF AWAY FROM THE EXTREMES

Balance, rather than taking it all away and depriving ourselves, is the essential ingredient that we should strive to remember daily with Lagom. If we spend our whole lives trying to deprive ourselves of the things we should and need to do, or the things that we enjoy, we will end up burnt-out. After burn-out, it's easy to head the other direction, swinging to the other side of the pendulum; this is not good for us either.

You Are Happier

Happiness can only begin when you have had a chance to get those basic needs taken care of, and it will end with the love and the gratitude of what your life is and is becoming. When you begin adding some of the principles of Lagom into your life, you will see the importance of making sure that the excess is gone, leaving room for more of the things that are wanted and needed. When things are just right, which is encouraged with the fundamentals and process of Lagom, you will feel good.

You Will Become Healthier

With Lagom, you will learn how to do more of the healthy things that you need with balance. You will learn how to reach the right amount of working out, rather than doing too much and wearing yourself out - or too little, skipping out entirely on the health benefits of exercise. It is possible to have too much of both, so learning how to balance these can be so important.

LAGOM IS A PART OF BEING MINDFUL

When we can learn how to become more mindful, we are learning how to become more aware of the things around us. It is as simple as that. To have the kind of moderation that is necessary to work with Lagom, we need to be mindful.

THERE CAN BE A LOT OF FULFILLMENT IN "JUST ENOUGH"

We live in a culture that is all about getting more and having more. We think that we need to have this thing and that thing. We go into debt to keep up with the neighbors and to have the best and the most of everything. This never makes us feel good for long; we will feel overwhelmed and tired and have to work more to pay off the things that we no longer need or even find happiness with. This is the exact idea that Lagom works towards fixing in our lives.

Lagom may be a process that seems somewhat foreign and new to a lot of us who are not from the country of Sweden, but it might be exactly what a lot of us will look for to improve our lives and find more happiness overall. It may take some shifting of your mindset and your way of living, but it is not as drastic and life changing as some of the other types of options that you can go with. That is one of the best outcomes that results from implementing Lagom in your life.

Chapter 3: Adopting the Lagom Mindset

If there is one thing about this kind of lifestyle that is truly inspiring and something that you should pick up on it is this: it is not about making things work less or work more. What this kind of paradigm is teaching us is that we should balance in all things and make things work better.

Do we get rid of beautiful furniture because they are less functional? No —what we need to do is to add beauty to functionality finally getting the necessary balance between these two aspects.

Why? It is because both beauty and functionality are important.

DIET, DIET, DIET

A Lagom lifestyle is big on caring for oneself. You will begin to be more self-conscious. That means you should acknowledge where you are at right now and do more to correct things so that you will live a healthy lifestyle.

A Lagom lifestyle entails maintaining a balanced diet. That means you will make a healthy choice to live healthy and to eat healthy. Does that mean you will no longer try different cuisines? No it does not.

Practicing Lagom allows you to treat yourself and enjoy life's pleasures. However, do not binge. Eat, drink, enjoy things but you should know when you have had enough; and when you do, then stop. Control—it's all about self-control. And that is one way how you can live a healthy and happy life.

Practicing Kindness

Another important facet of a Lagom mindset is the practice of kindness. That entails being kind to yourself first and then being kind to others as well. We all make mistakes and we learn to forgive by first forgiving ourselves.

This inner kindness to oneself can then translate to being kind to other people as well. Embracing a Lagom mindset will mean that you will take care of yourself because if you do then you will be empowered to take care of others.

It should be obvious that you can't help other people if you can't help yourself. You need to be standing on higher ground before you can pull other people up. The sense of community in a Lagom mindset is strong because the individual is better able to care for itself.

But that doesn't mean you will not practice the principle of sacrifice. when you come to a point when you want to put the needs of others like your friends and family above yours then you will do it. It is part of Lagom too—in fact it is a huge part of that mindset.

However, do take note that before you can sacrifice anything you must be fit enough to provide that necessary sacrifice. And that is the cycle of it all—one thing leads to the other.

This is also why Lagom is a very powerful concept in the workplace. Imagine a company where the culture is that there is no need for cutthroat competition for the next promotion at the end of the quarter. Imagine everyone from the rank and file to the top-level managers being united to move the business forward.

In that environment everyone benefits from the push that the company is getting. Because everyone does their part rowing the boat everyone gets to the shore safely and quickly. It's the perfect win/win setup.

SHOPPING FOR THE LONG TERM

They practice what is called a "capsule wardrobe" in Sweden. You may already be doing it and you just don't know, so here's how it goes.

Go through your wardrobe and find all the clothes that you haven't worn in a year. Take it off your wardrobe, wash and clean up those clothes, and then pack them so you can hand them down to someone who may benefit from it. Don't throw them away. Give them away to someone who may need them.

When you buy clothes don't just buy them because they're the latest fad. Be conscientious when you shop for clothes. Consider the quality of the item you are buying. Make sure that you are buying something that will last.

You can also practice this principle in the kitchen or with anything that you are buying. By being less of a hoarder or impulse buyer you are also helping the environment by reducing the amount of waste that you will one day throw away.

Chapter 4: Lagom in Relationships

It is even possible to put some Lagom in your love life! This is a place where a lot of people would like to see some improvement, but it is hard to find the right balance when starting a new relationship. You may be busy impressing the other person so that they are willing to go out with you and start a new relationship; this does not leave you with a lot of time to manage all the other things going on in your life at the same time.

It is a big balancing act to make everything work out the way that you would like, and even when a new relationship is started, you do not want to be stuck in the trap of having one thing take over all of the other aspects. In addition, with the ideas that come with Lagom, you will find that you can manage this a bit better, giving you a better chance at romance and a better love relationship overall as well.

KEEP THE DATES SIMPLE

This can go all the way to the kinds of dates that you have as well. While a fancy restaurant can be nice sometimes, having to do the greatest and the best each time is exhausting and expensive. Why not a walk and a picnic, or even just have a nice date night at home with homemade food and a nice movie? This helps to take some of the pressure off both of you and can be a great way to talk and get to know one another.

Remember with Lagom that it is all about the balance and how the two of you can create a possible new life together as a couple. In addition, if you start being out of balance in the first place, it becomes even harder to gain this balance back later on in the relationship.

Do Things that You Both Enjoy

As you are working on building up a new relationship, you must learn how to do things that both of you enjoy. You do not want to be the only one having fun on all of the dates or the other things that you do! You also do not want to be the one who is bored along the way either. When the two of you do things that you both enjoy, it is much easier to have fun and create a lasting bond that is so good for the relationship.

Take time out for each other

Your relationship has to fit into the balance with Lagom on occasion as well. Even if we do not mean for it to happen, sometimes the other distractions of the world and the other things that we need to take care of regularly will bring us down and can make it hard to do this. It is so important for a relationship to grow and flourish by spending time together, so start adding this as something important that needs to happen in your own relationship today to maintain that Lagom balance.

UNDERSTAND THAT "ALONE TIME" IS JUST FINE

Think of how much is being missed out on in the other parts of your life. Your work is likely suffering because all you can do is think about this other person. Your friends and family are getting pushed back and may feel a bit neglected and like they are not as important as this new person is, and they may feel a little left out and abandoned as well. While this is probably not what you had meant to do, it is something that can happen if you are not careful.

This does not mean that spending time with the new love interest in your life is a bad thing. it is necessary for the relationship to grow and flourish the way that you would like, and for both of you to learn a bit more about one another. However, when it becomes obsessive and includes the two of you only ever spending time with one another, then it is creating an imbalance that is not a part of Lagom.

Go at a Speed that is Right for Both of You

Sometimes, we are so caught up in the romance of something that we want to just jump right in and take full advantage of it to move things too quickly. When both parties want to do this and have settled on it being the best course of action for both of them, then this is just fine, and you can move ahead. Remember that the *just enough* can be different for each person, and for each couple as well. Maybe moving faster in the relationship is what works and is just enough for this couple, but maybe not.

Lagom & Friendship

Humans are social mammals. Whilst some people are more sociable than others, very, very few people have the nature to live alone, without any contact. For the vast majority of us, socializing with others is a human need alongside food, water, and shelter.

Nonetheless, despite our sociable nature achieving Lagom in our relationships is difficult. Often people feel like they are suffocated and surrounded with people, yet somehow not finding any meaningful relationships. Alternatively, people often find themselves lonely, not forming bonds or spending enough time with people altogether.

The key to finding Lagom in relationships is to firstly understand your personality and the difference between introversion and extroversion, which will help you, understand how you connect to people.

Introversion and extroversion are a spectrum, which in psychology, is defined by how much stimulation a person enjoys. Introverts are more sensitive to stimulation and therefore enjoy and thrive in lower-stimulation environments. As a result, introverts often enjoy spending time during low-key activities, such as reading, listening to music, or socializing with just a few close friends.

introverts can also enjoy more lively settings, but at the same time, find these activities draining. Someone with an introverted nature may enjoy going to a party or a concert but will find themselves feeling tired afterward and needing some time to relax in some low-key activities. Introverts recharge through low-stimulation activities, during which they feel most alive and awake, which are generally performed alone, but very good friends or family members can be involved too.

As a general rule of thumb, introverts tend to be more self-reflective. They reflect and dwell on their own mental states often and more likely to be concerned about how they are acting or thinking compared to extroverts.

It may be this self-reflective nature that makes social interactions more taxing; an introvert will be more likely to monitor their actions, thoughts, and feelings compared to an extrovert, which might make social interactions seem more daunting, whilst rewarding environments where introverts are alone or around people they feel comfortable with are more desirable and sought after.

Introverts enjoy focusing deeply on a single activity and they would rather observe or understand events from afar before joining. Introverts choose their relationships with much more care than others; they tend to have fewer friends and relationships, but these relationships typically involve a deeper bond with more trust involved.

Extroverts generally have more friendships and relationships than introverts, although most of these friendships will be less intimate. With that being said, extroverts are more comfortable and confident in friendships and relationships which involve less trust, which they tend to still find enjoyable and rewarding. Extroverts also tend to be enthusiastic and talkative by default.

Nonetheless, if you want to find Lagom in your relationships, it's important to understand where you fall on the introversion-extraversion scale. If you are an introvert, you might find yourself happier and more energetic cutting back on your social interactions and spending more time doing things you enjoy by yourself.

When you spend time by yourself, you might also find yourself enjoying your time more if you find yourself hobbies and activities you can focus deeply on - try writing, programming, or painting.

If you are an extrovert, it might be better to put yourself in situations where you can meet new people and occupy a greater portion of your week in company. Try to find hobbies which you can perform in a group or with friends.

Additionally, be aware of the types of commitment that other people make for you and whether or not you are taking this for granted. This type of awareness includes paying your fair share for events you are involved in, but also displaying gratitude for favors, even for simple things, such as someone offering to drive you somewhere or sacrifice their time for you.

On top of this, consider how much attention you require and how much attention you give to people. Are you someone who always talks about your own problems, but doesn't listen to the problems of other people? Do you need to be the center of attention and struggle when other people are in the limelight? Do you only listen to people to have your turn to talk, or do you reflect and consider what they are saying? Do you always dictate the plans, or do you let other people have a say when arranging when you meet and what you do? These are all examples of being too self-centered in a relationship; you need to be genuinely interested in what the other person thinks, feels, says and acts. They don't just exist to make you feel good.

The balance of giving and taking needs to be right for both parties. You need to give enough to keep your relationships healthy, but you also need to maintain friends and family bonds where people don't take too much.

If you have friends that constantly ask you for favors, but don't give them, who are self-focused but don't care too much about your life and constantly require you to arrange plans, then consider whether the friendship is worth it for you. Even if you appreciate them as a person, or enjoy their company, in some circumstances you might be better off alone. At the very least it's worth trying to express your feelings and the ways in which you are not happy with the relationship – if the other person values you, they will make an effort to change.

Naturally, all relationships are difficult and the circumstance at hand might alter the balance of giving and taking. There is no perfect balance for everyone; what matters is how the people involved feeling about it.

Some relationships can be quite one-sided in terms of attention given, favors and sacrifices made and the overall sense of equality between people, but nonetheless still feels fulfilling and balanced to the people involved.

A wealthy individual might want to spoil their lower-income partner with gifts and treats for example, but this can feel inappropriate depending on the understanding and relationship these partners have. Likewise, a quieter and self-reserved person might enjoy spending time with someone who is louder and self-focused, achieving a type of asymmetrical balance.

Chapter 5: Lagom Minimalism

As you make small cultural shifts into a Lagom lifestyle you will begin to understand that by owning a few things only you will feel healthier. You will feel some sort of release from all the clutter. It can even foster a brighter outlook in life.

Your point of view will slowly shift from that of focusing on material possessions to that of focus on things that are truly meaningful and lasting. This is no less than an appealing idea.

That is why this idea or lifestyle is gaining such a huge following. Some people call it Lagom, some call it essentialism, while others call it minimalism. However what people don't realize is that these three concepts are not synonymous.

Yes, Lagom is not exactly minimalism, minimalism is not essentialism, and essentialism is not Lagom. However they do have common features, which is why people use any of these terms loosely.

All things considered, we can say that Lagom and essentialism are the easier or softer versions of minimalism. Another way to put it is that Lagom has its own twist (a Swedish tweak?) on what mainstream minimalism is all about. We'll go over each of these concepts in the discussion below taking note of their differences as well as their similarities.

WHAT IS MINIMALISM?

Some people think of minimalism as living on bare bones belongings. You can even imagine empty rooms with very minimal furnishings and a family having only a few possessions.

Those maybe stark images that people imagine but minimalists aren't like that. The practice varies from one person to the next. there are extreme minimalists who do live on bare bones belongings but they aren't the rule when it comes to this philosophy.

Most people focus on the belongings that a person owns when they talk about minimalism. But it isn't all about owning less and being happy with it. It does apply that, yes, but it is more than that.

Minimalism's focus is on the core values of the individual. The actual focus is on what one wants out of this life. By owning fewer things one gets away from the distractions of wanting to own more.

The lifestyle focus of modern minimalism is only one way to practice this philosophy. A minimalist value and focuses on intentionality. That is why they only own that which is necessary. They intentionally focus only on the things that they need so that they can focus on the truly valuable things in life.

Lagom Version of Minimalism

In the Swedish version of minimalism, you don't necessarily have to go down to bare-bones levels. You will own less because you only want what is enough for you. You will emphasize simplicity in the things that you own and do.

However, you will also add a touch of coziness and comfort in your lifestyle. And that is not entirely bare bones as it were. In practice, you will also avoid overworking since that will put less emphasis on the other aspects of your life. A Lagomist will practice minimalism to the point where he or she has attained balance in life. You will practice owning less but putting emphasis on not having too much or too little. What you are aiming for is getting the things that are just right.

Practicing Lagom Minimalism in the Home

Now, practicing Lagom minimalism can't be done all in one day. That will depend on how much clutter you need to get rid of. It will entail a lot of sacrifices and you will feel like you're parting with some of the things that you are most emotionally attached to.

However, by taking the time and effort to practice Lagom in the home you will be able to find the most precious things in your life and focus on those things first. Note that you will undergo the deepest house cleaning you will ever do in your life.

Clear your schedule and allot at least 1 to 3 hours a day for 7 days.

DAY 1—CLOSETS

Start day 1 during the weekdays. You should allot day 6 and day 7 for the weekends. Trust me; you're going to need a lot of time during those last two days.

Day 1 decluttering should be easy enough. Your closets are the easiest to start with which is why most people begin with that.

Prepare three big boxes (or any size that will be big enough for you). One box should be labeled as the donate box, the second one will be labeled as the consignment box, and the last one is the throw-away box.

Now, here is the rule that we have talked about earlier in this book. There is only just one rule but if you want to add a few more additional rules for the sake of functionality (i.e. clothes that you may use in a future time) then you can add them.

Here is the rule again: if a piece of clothing or any clothing article hasn't been used or worn in a year then it should be removed from your closet. there are exceptions, which are the additional rules that we have mentioned earlier.

If you have a special suit or dress or maybe a costume that you may wear in the future (like a Spiderman costume or a tuxedo or maybe a gown that you reserve for special occasions) then they don't have to get taken down.

Now, here's another important rule—if it doesn't fit you anymore then it has to go away. Go through all the stuff in your closet and spare no drawers. Everything should be examined and evaluated.

You will end up with four groups of clothing articles:

Clothes that fit you, clothes that you will continue to wear this year, special clothing that you may use in the future – these will stay in your closet.

Clothes that still fit and still look dazzlingly good but you no longer use or wear – these clothes will go into consignment, something that you can sell somewhere or to a garage sale that you will want to do in the coming days.

Clothes that are in good shape but you don't want to sell (stuff that you think someone like a friend might want) – these will go to the donate box; always think of someone or maybe a charity to whom you will want to donate these clothes.

The rest, which includes the ones that don't fit you anymore or are just not wearable, will go into the box for throwing away.

Organize your closet after sorting. Bring the donations box to a charity or to the person you intend to give it away to. The ones for consignment should be taken to a thrift store or some place that will take them and then the ones for throwing away should be thrown away.

Do this immediately. Do not delay.

DAY 2—BATHROOM

The bathroom should be either the easiest place to organize or the second easiest. There should be a lot less stuff in the bathroom to organize. You can switch, do the bathroom on day 1 and the closet on day 2.

But it's all up to you. I just put the closet on day one since it will have a lot of emotional baggage—trust me it will. Those clothes will trigger a lot of emotions. It's best that you get rid of the emotional stuff first so that the rest of the process will be a lot easier.

Reorganizing your bathroom will be a lot easier since most of the stuff you'll find here can only be placed into two categories—for use and for throwing away. You will hardly find anything that you can recycle in the bathroom.

Makeup and hair products should go in a separate cabinet or drawer. Another option is to put all your usable hair products in one bin and the makeup in a separate container.

DAY 3—KITCHEN

The kitchen should be another easy spot to declutter. A lot of the stuff that you need to check would be hidden away inside cabinets. You might be surprised to find how creative you were when trying to fit everything in such small spaces.

At other times the clutter that you need to sort out will just be hidden in plain sight. Yes, they will be on your countertops. I suggest that you work with the cabinets first so that you can create more room in there for the stuff that you will need to use.

Remember, the same rules apply—if something looks like you have never used it in a year then you should toss it out. If something will never be used this year, then it has to go away as well. If something could be used sometime in the future (like a special Asian noodle maker for instance) that will be used in your anniversary or some other special occasion then store it.

You should decide which knives you're using in the coming months. Place the knives and other cutlery that you are no longer going to use in a separate box. Consider selling them or recycling them. Go through the other utensils and kitchen appliances and sort them out in this manner as well.

Pick the pots and pans that you will be using. There will usually some that you no longer use. Put them in a separate box and decide whether you will give them away or throw them away.

Make sure to separate the pots from the pans. The pots can be stacked and you can store the tops separately. That should help to get things organized.

Place the Tupperware, pots, pans, kitchen tools, countertop appliances, and other stuff in their separate shelves. The ones that have to go should be disposed of as soon as possible. Do this today or first thing in the morning.

Keep only as few countertop items as possible.

DAY 4—BOOKS, TOYS, AND ALL THE STUFF IN THE LIVING ROOM

On day 3 go over the stuff in your living room including all the toys, books, magazines, and other things that can be found there. Grab a basket (you can order cheap ones on Amazon) or repurpose an old container or box and put that by the staircase or in any area corridor where everyone usually passes by.

That box or container/basket is where you will put all the misplaced or otherwise lost items. When the box gets filled, place the items in the designated spot where they should be. Remember to throw away toys and any stuff that you or your kids no longer use.

DAY 5—BEDROOM

There should never be anything under your bed—nothing. They will just gather dust there. Dresser tops and cabinet tops should also be inspected, decluttered, and cleaned. Follow the same rules as before when sorting things out. Place a laundry basket in a corner that is hidden from view. That's where all the laundry goes.

DAY 6—BASEMENT AND ATTIC

Basement and attic day should be done on the weekend—maybe on a Saturday. You will spend more time here than on the other days. You should get some help when you sort things out on day 6.

Follow the same rules as before. Tents, fishing gear, and other equipment will have to be stored separately. The same thing is true for holiday decorations and other specialty items.

Day 7—Garage

Again, you might want to get some help when organizing your garage. You will follow the same rules as before, but you will need a few organizers to get the garage fixed up.

I recommend that you install shelves and peg boards up on the walls to help get things organized. Yard tools can be hung on the boards and the tools that don't fit in your toolbox should go into the shelves.

Lagom, Clutter, & Minimalism

The Lagom lifestyle seeks to find the goldilocks sweet-spot in every area of life; not too much and not too little. If you look around your house right now, you'll probably realize that this concept doesn't apply to your surroundings.

Most people are hoarders, accumulating far more possessions than they could ever want or need. Even without all the excess clothes, books, ornaments, films, games, toys, shoes (and so on), most people still have far too much furniture. There is a beauty and elegance in having an emptier room with just a few key pieces of furniture. A minimalistic room is calming, pleasant to be in and easier to keep tidy and clean.

To truly live Lagom, it's time to start getting rid of the clutter. A lot of people struggle deeply with separating themselves from their possessions, so it can be best to be slow and gentle in your approach when trying to separate yourself from your stuff.

Start by dipping your toes in the water and getting rid of any duplicate possessions. Often you might realize that you own multiple copies of the same book or film or that you own a bunch of clothes that all fulfil the same purpose. Do you need five pairs of gloves or six scarves? Likewise, if you comb through your kitchen, you'll probably recognize that you probably have too many frying pans, saucepans, cutlery or other equipment. Not only do you have too much, when you start to think about it, you'll probably realize that you only use just a few pans or plates and that you keep everything else around for the sake of it.

Another easy way to trim down on the clutter is to get rid of anything that is broken or faulty, especially if it's not required. Our sense of wastefulness encourages us to keep things until they are completely non-functional, but if you're not using it, then it's just getting in the way. This category includes things such as socks with holes, saucepans with broken handles, power tools that are no longer working and clocks which no longer tell the time. Make a concrete decision; either devote time and money to getting the item repaired, or let it go.

If you can cut down on your clutter using these two techniques, then you've made a good start, but there is usually so much more you can do!

Tackle the attic or garage, filtering through all the boxes you've put there to deal with sometime 'later'. Try to sort items into four categories; keep, sell, give and discard. Often junk ends up being stored just because we are too lazy to get rid of it at the time – we would rather just store something away than deal with it right there and then. this approach backfires on us; we not only have to deal with the junk later, but it takes up space in the meantime and can get in the way when we need to find something.

Anything that you don't want to keep but is too good to throw away is something you should be selling, or at the very least, giving away. Don't be lazy!

Selling things in the modern era isn't hard with the internet making the process only take a few moments. If you plan to sell, all you need to do is make a listing on a website such as eBay or Amazon. Take a few good quality photos of the items you are selling and make sure to include them in your listing. In the photos, the item needs to be visible, in bright light, from a few different angles and preferably against a blank background (and clean, mono-color area of carpet or surface will do).

Add a short, but clear and honest description of the item and then set a reasonable price. For someone to buy your item, it's going to need to be at an attractive price, but you should still be able to make a few dollars on most items worth selling. Be careful to think about the cost of postage in your price – you'll probably only want to sell to places within your country and you should look up the prices and dimensions of parcels to make sure you are charging enough to cover the costs and still make a small margin of profit.

Some items are unlikely to be sold for any real value. Most books are far too common and too cheap, to be worthwhile selling on most platforms. Likewise, larger objects such as most pieces of furniture will be too expensive and bothersome to ship anywhere and make money.

However, most charity shops and organizations are more than happy to take any quality goods off your hands for free, provided you are willing to move the items yourself. Through platforms such as Craigslist, or even popular social media groups on websites such as Facebook or Instagram, you can advertise that you are giving away stuff. If you include a good description, contact details, and a few good photos, you'll soon get a lot of interest – people like free stuff!

At this point, some people will feel successful in their attempts to declutter. However, for some people decluttering is more than just getting rid of junk, duplicates, and broken stuff. For these people, decluttering also involves learning how to use and need less altogether;

developing a lifestyle that revolves around fewer possessions.

However, Lagom is not austerity or a rejection of material things. Lagom is about living in moderation and achieving the correct balance of not too much or not too little. What is considered 'just enough' will vary person by person and for some people, this might simply involve having more possessions than others.

Nonetheless, it can be revealing to challenge yourself to look at all your possessions and think about which ones you truly need, and which ones truly make you happy. If we are honest with ourselves, you probably own a huge amount of stuff that doesn't contribute to your happiness and nor is it stuff that you need. Look at your house right now. What do you use on a weekly basis? What do you use daily? What would you notice missing if it suddenly disappeared?

If you suspect that you don't need something, but you're not willing to fully let it go, try storing it away for a month. If you forget about the item or realize that didn't need to use that item for the entire month, then you probably don't need it. At the very least, it probably isn't contributing to your happiness in any meaningful way.

One popular application of this concept has become known as the 'capsule wardrobe'. The capsule wardrobe involves limiting yourself to around 40 or so pieces of clothing, including accessories such as shoes or scarves. The capsule wardrobe is adjusted at the start if every season, with necessities such as warmer clothing being subbed in for summer clothing as the months grow colder. Everything else is stored away or sold.

Chapter 6: Living Life in Moderation with Lagom

In general, society teaches us to constantly search for new things. We move on to a new, hit T.V series after we have finished watching the last one on Netflix and we buy a new album only to become bored with it after listening to a few times. We are always on the lookout for tastier foods to eat, new clothes to wear, or new things to do.

Our gradual lack of interest in the things around us is due to how our brains react to stimulation. The first few times we perceive a stimulus our brains sharply focus on whatever stimulus we are perceiving, whether it be something we are watching on T.V or something we are eating, and it gives us a brief mental high.

Watching T.V. and browsing the internet are two of the best examples of this effect. Any program or show we watch on T.V is full of scenes and events that are constantly changing, hooking our brains to keep watching by triggering a stimulation reaction.

If you've ever felt that the T.V or show you are watching has a hypnotic pull on your mind, or that you find a background show hard to tune out, this is the reason why – the physiology of your brain is working against you.

Browsing through the internet has a similar effect. The internet is full of interesting and novel stimuli; from a constant newsfeed stream from Facebook to hordes of endless YouTube videos or massive websites such as Reddit, it's easy for the mind to get hooked on all the novelty.

However, somewhere along the way, you might realize that you are not enjoying yourself – you are only spending time on the T.V or the internet out of habit or instinct and that you are feeling quite bored or flat.

You might even want to pull yourself away or do something else but be struggling with the motivation to do so.

There are two ways you can choose to respond to this accustomization effect. The first method is to constantly seek new things and new experiences, which is the choice most people in Western society make by default.

Boredom is avoided by ditching the old and chasing novelty, wherever it might be. However, this approach has its limitations. There is a certain sense of desperation is constantly seeking new fleeting distractions from an otherwise boring or non-pleasurable life.

Like any addict, there is also an escalation effect – whatever we seek has to be more interesting and more engaging than the previous novelty, which eventually leads to us struggling to find something that genuinely interests us. Depending on your circumstances, you might also lack the means to constantly chase new things; the time and money just might not be available to try and keep your life feeling vibrant.

The second method is to learn to live in moderation and seek activities which are fulfilling by themselves. This approach is two-fold. By living in moderation and limiting the amount of time spent consuming media or doing 'entertaining' things, the acclimatization effect doesn't occur.

Our brains don't become accustomed to the things we do because we spend less time doing them. As a result, for the person who lives in moderation, when they do spend time watching T.V or browsing the web, they genuinely enjoy the experience – it still seems fresh and interesting.

The key here is balance – the person who lives in moderation might spend some time watching T.V, but they will only tune into the things that they are genuinely interested in. This type of person might watch a series like Game of Thrones, for example, looking forward to a new 1-hour episode per week. They are less likely to just watch T.V for the sake of it – browsing through hundreds of channels in the evening and settling for whatever seems the least boring.

The other half of this two-fold approach is seeking activities which are genuinely fulfilling. Instead of spending time on activities which we think are fun, but we typically admit bring us no real benefit (i.e. watching T.V.). A person who lives in moderation also adds things to their life which are inherently rewarding (such as learning a new skill, building new relationships or exercising).

Our interest in these activities doesn't fade over time – if anything these hobbies become richer and rewarding with the time, we spend doing them. Above and beyond spiritual platitudes, the way our brains react to these types of activities is genuinely different – instead of getting a momentary high from perceiving something new, our brains enter a 'flow' state, associated with increased concentration, greater energy and a sense of joy and creativity.

Likewise, spending time on your hobbies and other activities which generate a flow state or you find fulfilling is also associated with greater happiness in general. Research suggests that engaging with hobbies makes you more confident and more independent because it teaches you that you can achieve things in your life outside of your work.

There is often an excuse that we don't have time for hobbies, or anything outside of work and our responsibilities, but for most of us, if we challenge ourselves, we know this isn't true. It feels as if we don't have time because we are so used to wasting our time doing things we don't enjoy, that we never feel rested.

There are a few other habits and techniques you can embrace to help you live Lagom. Firstly, try spending time doing activities that are slow and that deepen your concentration. Western society is developing a love affair with meditation for this reason, but you don't have to sit cross-legged to recapture your attention. Anything that makes your mind work a little slower than its normal pace is good.

Our minds are used to quickly flicking through new stimuli, largely due to the nature of our fast-paced T.V shows, smart phones, and internet distractions and perhaps the speed expected of us during our working hours. As a result, some psychologists have suggested we are losing our ability to pay attention to anything for more than just a few seconds at a time – an effect that is detrimental to our ability to develop hobbies and find fulfilment.

So make an effort to deliberately fight this trend with anything that lets your mind slow down. Spend time walking outdoors in nature, reading a novel, painting or simply pausing for a moment to be mindful and aware. One blossoming example of a simple activity that can deepen your concentration is using a coloring-in book – in the past few years the sales of coloring books aimed at adults have exploded – at one point, demand w

Another method to find balance is to delay gratification. You can still enjoy luxuries, treats, and pleasures but the ability to control our impulses by delaying gratification is paramount. When we delay and restrict the things that give us pleasure, we enjoy them even more. For example, if you eat chocolate every day, you might enjoy it, but not nearly as much if you only ate it once a week or once a month. When eating something every day we become bored and used to it, but when eating it once a month, the sensation is more intense and fuller.

Finally, the last suggestion for finding Lagom is to focus on savoring whatever you are doing. If you are eating, focus on the flavors and textures of the food. If you are watching T.V., put away any distractions and pay full attention to what you are watching.

When you spend time with other people, engage in the conversation – don't just take their presence for granted. Savoring your current activity this way generally requires you to stop multitasking constantly. Put the smart phone down and don't eat whilst you watch T.V, study or work, or listen to music as you browse the web. Instead, do things one at a time, but take care to enjoy each thing as you do it. By focusing on the activity, you are doing, especially if it's enjoyable, you enrich your experience of things. You will feel more rested, relaxed and calmed because you are paying more attention to the experiences in your life that are pleasurable and rewarding.

Chapter 7: Adding Lagom into Your Home Life

The first place we will look to help you to make sure that Lagom is added into your life is in your home. You spend a good deal of your time in your home. You sleep there, enjoy time with your family, eat and cook there, take in some peaceful time, entertain, and feel safe and comfortable while you are in that area. It makes sense that you will want to spend some time adding some more Lagom into your life and you will want to start with this process in your own home.

To truly embrace Lagom, you're going to need to change the way you think about your house and the stuff you buy. Lagom involves a personal responsibility to the planet, but being environmentally friendly can also help save your wallet.

DECLUTTER THE HOME

To start with, decluttering your home can help to add in more of the Lagom as well. A simple and balanced home is one of the best ways for you to achieve a lifestyle that is considered Lagom. Not only does a lot of excessive décor all over the place start to contribute to the amount of anxiety that you feel (which can be bad for all parts of the body and mind), it is also going to block out some of your creativity, and can make it almost impossible for you and others in the home to relax.

CHOOSE WHITE OR GRAY

If you are looking to get started with a new painting project in your home, then changing the walls to gray or white is the best choice for you. Both shades are good for brightening up space and can allow for accent pieces and any other items that you choose for that room to start standing out. In addition, the color palette is muted can turn the home into a haven that is more relaxing to escape to after you finish up at work – or after completing all of the other obligations that you have during the day.

BE PROGRESSIVELY PURPOSEFUL ABOUT YOUR 'STUFF'

If Lagom is about control and aims a simple method to grasp it tends to be through looking at how much 'stuff' we have in our lives and making changes to our association with this stuff. Most of us purchase unmistakably more material things than we need, and often it's this gathering of things that worry us with more mess, also having a thump on sway on nature.

THINK ABOUT THE INTENSITY OF BALANCE

I get that even only the word 'balance' can sound exhausting and not particularly fun, yet there is a sure influence in grasping it, particularly around food and spending (there are numerous connections between our association with food and our association with cash!) I don't generally think balance comes that effectively to us, yet when you start deliberately thinking about what balance may resemble for you around your eating regimen and spending it very well may be incredibly useful.

Start by thinking about what different parts of the bargains may resemble, what might totally over liberal eating closely resemble you? How might very prohibitive eating closely resemble you? At the point when you take a gander at boundaries you truly can perceive how magnificent control can be, it's the Goldilocks 'without flaw' feeling!

SPARE BEFORE YOU SPEND

Nowadays it's truly normal to whack everything on a Mastercard however that in itself isn't entirely manageable. Take a stab at sparing before you spend! At the point when you start sparing it can likewise imply that you by and large become progressively mindful of your ways of managing money and spending plan and that is got the chance to be something worth being thankful for!

CHECK-IN WITH YOUR WORK/LIFE BALANCE

Is it accurate to say that you are completing work on schedule? Taking your mid-day breaks? Browsing messages on the ends of the week? Lagom is about parity and working constantly allowing for play or unwinding isn't healthy or supportable over the long haul. How might you change parts of your lifestyle to make it more adjust?

SURVEY YOUR HOMES ECOLOGICALLY FRIENDLY STATUS

Being progressively mindful of the earth and our effect on it is undoubtedly Lagom. Are there any progressions you can make around your home to reduce your effect? This may be changing all the lights to vitality sparing ones, adding a protecting evaporator coat to your high temp water heater, starting a manure load and being increasingly mindful of the food squander you make.

LESSEN YOUR ALTERNATIVES

Your early introduction of 'diminishing your choices' strength be a negative one yet let me clarify. Nowadays we need to make incalculable choices every day. From the minute we get up we need to choose what to wear, what to have for breakfast, to stroll to work or take the transport, to make a pressed lunch or get it around. While having a few alternatives is an incredible thing, having too many can leave you feeling overpowered and destroyed of vitality.

ADDING LAGOM INTO YOUR PARENTING STYLE AND RELATIONSHIPS AT LARGE

To put it simply, Lagom isn't making do with less; it's finding the best framework to get incredible outcomes for everybody, concurring that said framework is the favored decision, and making simple to receive the rewards of it. It's not to no end that Sweden brags one the most commended social welfare frameworks on the planet.

TAKE BREAKS

Research shows that ordinary breaks make you more joyful, however they advantage your work as well. Regardless of whether for making up for lost time with associates or getting some natural air, normal breaks will add equalization to each part of your life.

GET A BICYCLE

Exercise in the entirety of its magnificence – in Sweden, the word 'movement' drives the route to a gentler, low-support approach to remain well. With new propensities that fuse a touch of development and outside air into your everyday life, you get the chance to raise that heartbeat normally without an expensive exercise center participation.

JOIN A FREECYCLE GATHERING

Squandering is a sin in Sweden, the nation that places well in each natural list possible, and what could be more Lagom, than ensuring that your never again adored things get the chance to be cherished again by another person – limiting waste, however utilization as well?

GO ON AN FLEA BINGE

Scarcely any individuals are as house pleased as the Swedes, however unlimited excursions to IKEA are a long way from perfect for the earth, and they can let you down regarding individual style and coziness factor as well. Swap meets are colossal in Sweden and have been for quite a while. Best of all: notwithstanding reused deals brimming with character, they give a chance to a day from screens and cutoff times, encompassed by companions, nature and old stories – regardless of whether you get back flat broke.

FIGURE OUT HOW TO REUSE

Grasp the joys of a pasta made of the stuff that was going to hit the container, and the fulfillment that accompanies what feels like a free supper because of a smidgen of inventive exertion. Thrifty cooking ticks pretty much every Lagom box: it's simple, it sets aside both time and cash, and – maybe in particular – it decreases food waste.

LOVE THY NEIGHBOR

Individuals who feel that they have individuals they can depend on are more joyful; trust is a significant factor in general life fulfillment rankings. With a long convention of apartment complex coops, it does not shock anyone that Swedes are great at the nearby network stuff. Set up a road party, start a vehicle pool, or simply offer to walk your neighbor's canine or water their blooms. A touch of benevolence goes far and can make you feel more secure, more joyful and more established.

PRACTICE GENUINENESS

Swedes are a country of not many words, and some discover their obtuseness inconsiderate. The flipside, notwithstanding, is a genuine responsibility to the trustworthiness and a refusal to participate in casual discussion, which carries with it an invigorating clearness. Find some kind of harmony and remain kind yet think before you talk. By naming things for what they are and jettisoning gracious decorations, you can limit false impressions and enjoy further, less confused relationships.

JOIN A CLUB

The drawback of a functionalist way to deal with language is that occasionally, you may need to join a club to meet new companions. The upside of such get-togethers is that they unite similarly invested individuals, support your work-life balance by accentuating that extra time of yours, and help imagination both at home and at work.

MAINTAINABLE HAPPINESS EVERYDAY

Keep in mind – happiness the Lagom path isn't tied in with being euphorically happy. Without a doubt, those minutes are to be treasured yet it's not how we're going to feel each moment of consistently.

It's tied in with enabling ourselves to arrive at a feeling of happiness – accomplish a greater amount of what makes us happy, give ourselves the opportunity to dream, develop kinships, spend an additional couple of minutes tasting that superbly fermented mug of coffee.

BRING SOME MORE NATURE INTO YOUR HOME

Just having one plant in your home is a great way to help reduce how stressed out you feel. Even if there are not a lot of sunny windows in your home to support a plant, some great plant options that you can use are not going to require the same kind of upkeep as others. Options that you can choose to add into your home to follow this principle of Lagom and to make sure that you are using plants that thrive with even a limited amount of sunlight includes Madagascar dragon trees, leaf fig trees, spider plants, and aloe vera plants.

LET IN SOME OF THAT NATURAL LIGHT

To achieve this kind of lighting, you can go with sheer window curtains and windows that are unobscured. These are good ways to make sure that as much of that natural light can get into the home as possible. If you are worried about how much privacy that you will have, but you would still like to follow along with this part of Lagom, you can look for light and thin drapes that will let in some of that natural light that you want. You can also invest in some rolling blackout blinds for the nighttime so you can let tha light in during the day and get more sleep at night.

MAKE SURE THAT THE OBJECTS IN THE ROOM CAN BREATHE

As much as possible, try to set single items so that they apart from one another to give them some breathing space as well as the spotlight that they deserve. When you are doing some décor in Lagom, each object needs to either serve a purpose or to delight you in some manner. In setting them apart from one another, it allows the room to feel less cluttered and makes it easier for you to appreciate the beauty and the purpose of each piece along the way.

USE SOME CANDLELIGHT WITH A NICE WARM GLOW

It is important to fill your home with candles in places where you would like to add in a touch of light, such as in the center of the table or a dark corner. Work to balance the space, and make sure that shelves or another location is not cluttered with too many candles in one place. Strive for equilibrium in your use of candles; instead of using too many in one place – or all over the place – set aside your extra candles so you will always have some on hand.

LEARN TO SLOW DOWN AND GET OUT OF THAT RUSH

We always rush, don't we? In this modern world we tend to rush as soon as we open our eyes. It is as if the world has pre-programmed our lives to go quickly by getting one thing done at a time. Sometimes rushing is part of the routine. You sometimes don't notice that you are already doing it robotically—it's almost automatic.

MIX TOGETHER SOME OF THE MODERN AND THE VINTAGE

When searching for some of the décor and vintage furniture that you want to work with, make sure to have some patience. Measure out the space that you would like to fill, and then make sure that you are flexible in the process. You could go into a store and be imagining that you want one piece in your head, and then find that you run across something that is much better instead.

There are a lot of things that you can do in your Lagom home to make it more comfortable and to ensure that it is "just enough" to make you happy. Follow some of these tips to help you clear up your home and get it all comfortable and ready to go, and you will be well on your way to implementing more of the Lagom philosophy in your own life.

Chapter 8: Adding Lagom into Your Workplace

The Lagom lifestyle understands that there needs to be the correct balance between your working life and everything else, a balance which is growing more precarious as Western workplaces are challenged by recessions, competitiveness, and globalization.

People can only work so hard for so long before the signs of wear and tear inevitably begin to show, with cracks in physical and mental health materializing. However, the drive and motivation to improve oneself, do a good job, and not shy away from difficulty are all good traits too. We need to fall into neither extreme but find the best middle ground; Lagom.

But how can we tell if we are working too hard or whether we are just being a little lazy? One of the best ways is to consider whether the number of hours you work is preventing you from thriving in other areas of your life. Do you still find time to spend with friends and family? Do you have enough time to exercise and cook? Do you devote time to hobbies and crafts that you find rewarding? If you are answering no to these questions and the reason is a sheer lack of time, then perhaps you should think about making an effort to achieve a better work-life balance.

There are various steps you can take to this end. Firstly, it's important to communicate to your company when the demands are too much or too unreasonable. In larger companies, upper management may not be aware of the demands placed upon lower level employees, whereas in smaller, flexible organizations rescheduling or reorganizing workloads can be easier.

Overall, whilst it may be a dangerous choice in some hostile workplaces, you'd be surprised at just how often employers and employees can find a compromise in regard to working hours.

It can also help to think more carefully about how you work. Long working hours can be the result of inefficiency and poor planning, such as prioritizing the wrong tasks or simply taking too long to achieve something.

Also, ensure that there is a clean cut between your working life and your home life. With the prowess of modern communication technologies, such as email and text-messaging, it can be difficult to distance yourself from the pressures of work.

Yet having some time in your life where you can relax without thinking about the problems in the office is key for good mental health. So try things like avoiding checking your emails in the evening, or refusing to take work-related calls during non-working hours. If you must work whilst you are in your home, try to designate a specific room as your office or study. It will be easier to get into a working mind-set whilst you are in that room, while also being easier to forget about work outside it.

If your working hours do limit your free time, ensure you sacrifice the right type of activities. Prioritize things which keep you mentally healthy and happy, such as exercise and friendships, over leisure activities that are more trivial (such as watching T.V).

Activities such as exercise or good social support function as protective factors, making you more resilient to the pressures of work and difficult, stressful events in your life. On top of this, account for all the hours associated with your work. Even if you work eight hours in a day, an hour-long commute both ways is still a commitment to your workplace. Likewise, tasks, such as delivering items, studying, research or working through lunch can all increase your workload, even if they don't fall within what you'd consider your normal working hours.

To help achieve Lagom in your work-life balance, you most first properly account for all the work you do.

you might find yourself on the opposing end of the spectrum; knowing you aren't working hard enough.

Perhaps you are not working as many hours as you should be, or when you are working, you're aware that you are not putting as much effort into your tasks as you should be.

Seek role models and inspiration from the people you know and try to hold yourself to their standards.

However, regardless of the social circles you keep, you still need to fully convince yourself to work hard initially. You need to find a reason or a cause to justify working hard and this reason needs to be a strong internal drive.

You might only desire to work hard to earn more money, but by thinking about the reasons why you want more money can still lead to the motivation to push yourself. If you have a family you need to support, think about them and how much you care for the well-being and their needs. If you need or want money for yourself, consider what you plan to do with it, or how it could improve your life. Dwell on these reasons and let the emotions that fuel them come to the surface.

Any employer who would like to create a place of work that is innovative and collaborative amongst all of the employees could take some tips from the Swedish idea of

Lagom. The idea of "just the right amount" means that we need to favor things like collectiveness, balance, and moderation over hierarchy, overwork, and individualism. It may be quite a bit different than what we will see in an American culture, but it is still an appealing proposition to work with.

Being able to achieve a sensible balance between work and life for all employees is important for any business, whether they are in Sweden, in America, or in many of the other countries on this planet.

Keep the work weeks to a minimum. When it comes to Lagom, the 60 hours or more a week idea needs to disappear. No one is benefiting from this. It is simply resulting in employees who are worn out and tired, and who aren't performing as well as they should. Limiting the hours to 40 hours will be plenty for most companies and can result in employees who are more willing to go above and beyond when the time calls for it with their employer later on.

Allow for some time to work at home. Sometimes, life comes up, and employees will need to be at home with a child, with their spouse, or because their car broke down. Forcing them to take days off and miss out on paychecks because of these life events can add to a level of stress that is not good for them, or for your business. They miss out on money they need for bills, and you miss out on some of the productivity that is needed.

Some businesses have started becoming more open in terms of the amount of time they allow their employees to work at home. This isn't possible for every business all the time and, you may have to outline times when the employee needs to make it into work. That said, allowing some flexibility can ease the stress that your employees have, and can help you to still get the work done that you need.

Instead, allowing the employees to have some say in the planning and in the metrics that are used can make a big difference. This will ensure that they can bring up some of their own concerns with the metrics that are being used and can help to ensure that the things that are being done will improve your business. You may be surprised by how much work can be done when you are not stressing employees out as much in the process.

Allow for a safe and open environment for everyone. Everyone in the company needs to feel like they are valuable. Making them feel like they are only there to make the company money and making it a big deal when they have to take time off, when they ask a question, or when they make a valid opinion, can be detrimental to the employee, and to your business. Your business cannot run without the employees, so why treat them as if they should be machines that have no opinions or private life outside of the workplace.

Consider listening to all employees when making decisions. Realize that your employees have - and want to have - a life outside of work. Employees like to go home and not have to worry about work. They want to have more time to go out, see friends, visit family, and spend time with their spouse and their kids. If you are trying to add more Lagom into your life, this is the kind of job that you need to look for. Even if it may not be the highest paying job, finding one that allows you to take a breather, and not have to think about and do work all of the time, rather than the things that you want to do, can help to improve your life and make it so much better overall.

Chapter 9: Lagom and Your Diet

How can you find Lagom in your diet? Western society is notoriously on the larger size, so we are not achieving the right balance in how much we eat, but perhaps the idea of Lagom can help us here.

In general, most diets are harsh and focus on an abstinence or deprivation of the foods we like to eat. This is not Lagom! To truly live in moderation, we need to embrace a slice of cake every now and then and be happy to gorge ourselves, on occasion. By failing to moderate our diets and trying to be too strict with our approach to health, we end up causing more damage through yo-yo dieting.

Driving this response is that defeated feeling that if the diet is already broken, you might as well go 'all-out' and enjoy yourself, or sneak in as much junk food before you officially start your diet again. Alternatively, for those of us who are emotional eaters, the disappointment of breaking our diet may cause us to resort back to binge eating as a habitual way to cope with our feelings.

We typically feel that it's our fault for breaking diets and that we should just try again. However, perhaps a different approach might be more successful. Strong innate desires drive us to eat and resisting these urges is difficult. If you have struggled with your weight or diet before, try taking a more balanced approach; allow yourself unhealthy food every now and again, but just don't go overboard.

Instead of seeing a diet as a black and white set of rules and limitations, try interpreting with a dose of Lagom; it's okay to break the rules every now and again and it's better to let yourself have a few treats than breakdown and eat far too much.

It's important to note that the what-the-hell effect is not just limited to food but can be applied to various areas of your life, including money or telling the truth.

If you've set yourself a budget and break it, you are more likely to spend much more than you initially set out. Likewise, if you've made a pact to yourself, to tell the truth, and you let out a little fib, you tend to fall back into habitual lying. Susceptibility to the what-the-hell effect is a personality trait; if you are more likely to fall prey to this effect in your diet then you are vulnerable in your finances and other aspects of your life too.

As a result, to live Lagom, it's important to set realistic goals. In terms of dieting, you could allow yourself one unhealthy treat per day, or one day of the week where you can eat anything you want. In terms of budget, you can set aside a fixed amount for frivolous spending per week.

Better yet, research demonstrates that it's better to set a specific type of goal, called an acquisitional goal. For example, if you wanted to lose weight, it would be better to set the goal that you want to lose 10 lbs. rather than claiming you're only going to eat 1500 calories per day.

In both goals, the aim is to lose weight. However, with the latter goal, it's easy to feel like a failure the moment you've exceeded that magical 1500 calorie limit. With the former goal, there is no direct way to fail; you can drift further away from achieving the goal, or take longer to achieve the goal, but as long as it's physically possible for you to lose that weight, then you can still succeed. By framing the goal in a way where failure isn't possible, you can avoid the pitfalls of the what-the-hell-effect.

Similarly, it's also wise to avoid goals which tell you to stop doing things. The concept of **not doing** something is difficult for the human mind to process – our minds are built to think about things rather than to not think about things. the very idea of not thinking about something is strange and difficult, to begin with. In psychology, this effect has been observed in a phenomenon called the 'white polar bear effect'.

In a more realistic example, consider being on a diet and trying to avoid eating the biscuits in the cupboard. You can say to yourself that you shouldn't eat the biscuits, but by thinking about the biscuits, to begin with, you are already tempting yourself. The more you think about the biscuits, the more you tempt yourself. You are setting yourself up to fail.

Instead of trying to not think about the biscuits, a better strategy is to think about something else. By distracting yourself, you can forget about the biscuits altogether and not be tempted in the process. Similarly, by setting yourself a goal to do something else, instead of inhibiting your actions, you also avoid the type of intrusive thinking that makes you susceptible to falling prey to your temptations. For example, when you are hungry, instead of trying to avoid eating biscuits, or any type of junk food, try drinking a large glass of milk. Milk is quite filling, cheap and relatively low in calories – research has shown by drinking 400ml of milk in the morning, people tend to eat less throughout the day, therefore consuming fewer calories and losing weight. By setting the goal of drinking milk, you are not thinking about the biscuits at all, instead, you are thinking about milk, bypassing the temptation altogether. This type of positive goal setting demonstrates the power of Lagom in action. It's not about heavily restricting yourself but seeking a comfortable and better middle ground. On the same vein, if you do struggle, even with a positive goal don't be too strict on yourself and learn to forgive yourself when you break rules. More importantly, if you do break your diet, budget or any set of restrictions placed on yourself, understand that it's only a temporary setback. Getting too upset or too angry with yourself isn't Lagom; understand that it's okay to be disappointed, but you can still feel positive about the future too.

Lagom is something that you can work with when it comes to your eating choices. The American way of eating is not something that the rest of the world will share. Most countries will practice some more moderation when it comes to the amounts and types of foods that they eat.

When it comes to how you should eat, and eating well, Lagom means that you should find balance; this means having an awareness of what your body needs, learning how to find your cues of satisfaction, and gauging how you feel as you are eating. This keeps things healthier and moving along better than eating until you are stuffed or only eating because it is time to eat, rather than what we think we should eat or whatever is on the plate.

The Swedes are often all about everything being in the right amount, but this does not mean that they are afraid to treat themselves at times either. One only needs to take a look at all of the candy bins that are on the walls of all the stores in Sweden to see this. However, those who live in this country have a system for the treats, and they know when to treat themselves, and when to eat in a healthier manner.

Another thing to learn when it comes to eating with the idea of Lagom is that you do not have to fear fat. Letting go of a lot of the myths that are popular in America and eating things that have healthy fats in them can be a hard thing for many Americans who are worried about their diets and how healthy they can be. Still, this is something that you need to move past when it comes to eating in a balanced way on this kind of diet plan.

Even with this higher level of fat intake, it does not seem like the Swedes are overeating or gaining a lot of weight. This is because the right kinds of high-fat foods tend to be more satisfying, and good at helping you to not overeat, compared to some of the lower-fat options. If you learn how to listen to some of your own satisfied cues and do not take this too far, you would be able to lose weight and stay healthy the whole time, even when are eating foods that are higher in fat.

In addition to eating foods that are higher in healthy fats, you also need to make sure that there are a variety of grains present in your diet. there is the regular kinds like rice and wheat, but when it comes to the type that most Swedes like to consume, rye is king in that country.

Eating lots of healthy fruits and vegetables can make a lot of difference in the kinds of health that you will have as well. Try to add in some variety along with the other two food types that we have discussed. These will provide your body with a ton of great antioxidants and nutrients that the body needs and can be a great way for you to get something sweet without having too much through the week and ruining the kind of moderation that you need.

Lagom will help us to slow down and listen to our bodies about how much to eat. If you are eating too quickly, it is hard to know when you are done with eating, and when you have had too much. Remember that Lagom is all about *just enough*, so you should eat just enough to make the stomach happy and provide your body with the nutrients that it needs, and nothing more. But how are you supposed to know when you reach that point in eating if you have not slowed down enough to feel it?

Lagom will help us to enjoy our meals. Instead of going through and just scarfing down the food that you have all the time, without tasting it or even remembering what you ate from one meal to the next, Lagom asks you to slow down and get a chance to eat your meal and enjoy it. This is so important for anyone who is trying to be healthier overall, and it can make the whole idea of eating more enjoyable.

Slowing down, tasting the food that you eat daily, and being more mindful will make a big difference. You will enjoy the food that you are eating. You will slow down quite a bit and enjoy the mealtime as well. In addition, you will find that when you can slow down a bit, you can tell when you are satisfied, rather than overeating and then feeling – when it is too late - that it is time to stop.

Lagom will ensure that we eat more healthy foods that are better for us. Lagom is not against the occasional treat. However, this does not mean that you should have so many treats that you are not being able to watch the foods that you are eating along the way. Your diet should consist mostly of healthy foods, with lots of good protein, good whole grains and options, healthy fats, and good fruits and vegetables along the way. If you can eat these regularly, you can then have treats on occasion – without the guilt!

Lagom allows us to turn our meals into a more social event, rather than hurrying through them. If you are used to eating alone all of the time, or you are used to eating at a desk while doing work, you probably already know that this is bad for a lot of different reasons. You are alone, which can be a bit depressing and does not allow you to get any socialization in. In addition, since eating at your desk often means that you are working at the same time; this means you are not getting a break in the process.

No matter what meal you are eating, Lagom encourages it to be a social event. Sit down as a family and enjoy the breakfast together before you head off to school and work. Take some time during the workday to sit down with others in the office and talk, without excluding anyone, and be sociable. At night, either eat with your family or invite a friend over to enjoy a meal with you. These meals are not just about feeding the body and getting some nutrition in; they are also about taking a break from your day and improving your mental and emotional health AND becoming more social, all rolled up into one.

Lagom allows our meals to be more mindful. When we learn to focus on what we are eating in our meals we become more mindful of the food we are taking in. Take time to plate some of your meals rather than eating out of Tupperware or out of a bag. This helps the food (think fresh) as well as helping us to stop and enjoy the meals that we eat. Changing this one habit makes it easier to slow down and know when we are full, or when we are eating simply because food is in front of us.

It is important through this process that we learn how to listen to our bodies. In America, we see what the time is on the clock, and then assume that it is time for us to eat, whether or not we are feeling hungry at the time. When we fill up our plate, the plate is usually very large, and we feel like we need to eat every last bit, and sometimes go back for seconds.

While these things will help us to stay on a schedule, they are not very conducive to helping us learn the signs and signals that our bodies are sending out, and it often causes us to eat excessively much. It's easy to see the truth in this concept; look at the rise of obesity and the epidemic that it is causing in America, and we see that this is true.

The good news is that there are a few ways that you can change up your eating habits to make them fit in more with the ideas of Lagom instead of sticking with the bad eating habits that you already have. To start, go with a smaller plate at mealtimes and do not fill the plate to the rim; this alone can cut hundreds of calories and will make you feel full when you are done.

Chapter 10: Improve your Holidays and Celebrations with Lagom

No matter how much you like Christmas and all of the holiday spirit that comes with it, it is easy to admit that it has been taken over by commercialism – in other words: buying lots of stuff! Millions of Americans go into so much debt to celebrate Christmas and all that comes with it, and this leads to many problems down the line.

The first issue is how much is spent on presents. There is a whole weekend, Black Friday and the days after it, that is devoted to big deals on Christmas presents, and trees are often filled to the brim with lots of different items for everyone in the family. Presents need to be bought for every person in the family, and even for some friends and coworkers and teachers and everyone else. It can cost a small fortune buying all of these presents, and many times even with all of the money spent, these presents will be forgotten about, broken, or in the way in just a few weeks. The presents are not the only thing to be concerned about when it comes to the hassle with Christmas though. How much is spent on the lights around the house? How much is spent on a tree or on decorating the house, on all those Christmas parties, and all of the other festivities that come around this time? And how much time and money are spent to get all that food cooked and prepared to go see family and friends?

It is not that we do not enjoy these kinds of things, but it all sounds pretty exhausting, too. By the time the holiday is over, we all need a vacation from it, and our bank accounts are so drained that it takes most of the year to fix it and try to get things back in line. There has to be a better way to enjoy the good stuff of the holiday, without having such a mess to deal with along the way.

The good news is here that there are some other things that you can do to add more Lagom into your holidays as well. Adding this into your holidays may seem like you are a bit of a Grinch, but if it helps to maintain your sanity along the way, takes away some of the stress, and helps you to keep to some of your budgets from being busted, then it is something that is worth your time.

With this in mind, and remembering that we want to spend more of our time enjoying what is allowed in this holiday, rather than having to stress out and worry the whole time, we need to take some time to look at the different ways that you can add in more Lagom into your Christmas and the other holidays that are in your life as well.

CHRISTMAS CARDS

There are a few different steps that you can take to handle these Christmas cards. Some people decide that Christmas cards have to be sent out to everyone in their family, and their friends and coworkers and other people they have not seen or talked to in years. They will make or find the best cards, send out hundreds of cards, take family pictures, get stamps, and so much more.

CHRISTMAS DECORATIONS

The next thing that you can focus on to help out with the holiday season is with the decorations that you use during this time. If you want to go with Lagom, you would choose to not have many kinds of decorations up at all, or just the minimal, like a tree and a few lights. However, some people are into this holiday and enjoy having some more decorations around to celebrate. This is fine, but we need to find some simple and practical methods of doing this to ensure that we can see the results and not have to go into debt or struggle at the same time.

WRAPPING PAPER

An idea that is much better for you is using brown paper to make your own wrapping paper. You can recycle this later. Consider adding some tinsel or using some pretty string; use your imagination to help make your own wrapping paper unique and unusual. Doing this adds a personal touch, giving a unique look that you are not able to find with any of the commercial wrapping papers that are out there.

THE MEAL

If you are having a meal at your home for the holiday or throwing your own kind of holiday party, then it is likely that the sheer amount of work that you have to put into it will seem overwhelming. It can get expensive to spend your time getting plates, decorations, silverware, nice things for the whole process, and to make all of the meals, desserts, and sides that you would need to have a nice party

CHRISTMAS PRESENTS

The final thing that we need to take a look at when it comes to adding Lagom into your holiday time is with the Christmas presents. When it comes to these, we need to take a step back and consider whether we need to go all out and buy so much for the year? How many of those items do we need? In addition, are some gifts that are used regularly by your friends and family and your kids, or is it something that is thrown out and never used again?

Yes, it is always a lovely idea to give and receive gifts, but maybe it is time to consider the giving that we are doing, and not just give out presents for the sake of it. This ensures that the gifts that we do give are more meaningful, useful. Another advantage to thinking through the idea of present-giving: this helps us avoid just picking out the first item we see, spending too much money, in the process.

Chapter 11: Managing your Emotions with Lagom

Perhaps the most important place to find Lagom is inside your own head. Even if everything else is right, it's impossible to be happy if you are trapped in cycles of negativity. It doesn't matter if you have every material need covered, family and friends at your side or even a pleasant lifestyle if you cannot find inner peace and balance.

The most important part of maintaining a healthy and happy state of mind is to realize that your thoughts and behavior can be changed through effort and practice. Keeping positive is a skill that takes time to learn, but when mastered can be applied almost continuously.

Negative thoughts and feelings can rapidly spiral out of control and become all consuming. Small irritations and frustrations, for example, can rapidly sour our day, even though in truth, they do not matter.

We all know someone who is susceptible to road rage; someone who gets irrationally angry when they see someone driving too fast, too slow or in such a way that doesn't meet our high standards. As a result, the small task of driving anywhere can become a source of bitterness and anger that can last throughout the day.

You might not suffer from road rage, but most of us will have triggers that cause us unnecessary grief. We might dwell on how people are rude to us, how we are unhappy with our appearance, intelligence or our lack of popularity. A simple negative thought can poison our mood and over time, they can contribute to illness such as depression and anxiety. Whilst most of us will experience some degree of personal difficulty throughout our lives, most people in the Western world are fortunate to be in a position where their needs are met; they are educated, safe and enjoy civil liberties.

We shouldn't brush aside genuine problems when they occur, but we should take it upon ourselves to recognize our good fortune and the trivial, superfluous nature of most of the difficulties we face on a day-to-day basis.

Although most of us will appreciate this wisdom to some extent, that doesn't make it easy to apply. There is a wide gap between how we know we should feel and act and the way we do, a gap that may be able to be crossed through intention alone. Therefore, we should make an effort to cross this gap through special techniques and tips, helping us achieve a wholesome state of mind.

MINDFULNESS PRACTICE

To start with, try to develop a meditation practice. Small periods of mindfulness meditation have been demonstrated to help increase positivity, reduce stress and help battle depression and anxiety.

You don't have to try and find enlightenment, enter a trance or embrace any spiritual, religious or supernatural claims to benefit from meditation. Mindfulness meditation is simply an exercise in awareness and concentration, which can help us relax, energize and become aware of our thought patterns and behavior.

In mindfulness meditation, the meditator focuses on the breathing and the sensation of inhaling and exhaling the breath as it enters and exits the nose. Whenever a different thought or sensation arises, the meditator acknowledges it, becomes aware of the thought or sensation, and then returns to the breath. This way, the sensation of breathing functions like an anchor, helping the meditator to avoid becoming lost in thought or overwhelmed by emotion.

Generally, when practicing mindfulness meditation, most people become immediately aware of two things. Firstly, they recognize that their minds are very busy and that there is a constant stream of thoughts which serve no purpose.

Secondly, mindfulness meditation can also help reveal how limited our concentration and awareness is; it's hard to focus and clear your mind for even a few seconds.

Through returning the attention to the breath, the meditator can attempt to reach a state of calm, where the mind becomes less busy and their concentration deepens. Eventually, through learning how to reach a state of calmness and concentration, the meditator then can apply this state of mind to their lives, moderating their thought and behavior and learning to recognize thoughts and actions that are harmful to them and those around them.

It's important that when practicing mindfulness meditation, that the meditator doesn't attempt to control the breath or its rhythm but allows it to flow naturally.

The breath is such a fantastic focal point for awareness because it responds to our moods and feelings. If we are stressed or angry, the breath can become short, terse and painful. If we are relaxed and calm, the breath can become deep, free and soothing.

By focusing on the breath, not only can we become more aware of what we are currently feeling, but we can relax our minds and bodies through eventually allowing the breath to settle and become deeper of its own accord.

It's also important that you don't attempt to follow, dwell or chase any thoughts that occur. It's hard to translate or fully describe the difference between observing thoughts and feelings that pop-up and lingering on these thoughts, but most of us intuitively understand the difference.

Let the thoughts occur and monitor how your mind responds to them, but don't think about them any more than that. Imagine you are watching your thoughts flow down a river; you observe them as they pass, but you don't follow they flow downstream.

Meditation is usually performed in a position called the half-lotus position, where you sit on the ground or a meditation cushion and each foot rests on the opposing thigh. As a general rule, though, the position you attempt to meditate in is much less important than how much effort you apply or how consistently you meditate.

Any position that is comfortable, but also helps you stay focused and awake is desirable. Lying down in your bed is usually avoided for this reason – it makes it easy to fall asleep or simply daydream. However, many people perform meditation in kneeling postures or sitting down in an upright chair, so you can try different positions and see how they feel for you.

Meditation can be performed for any length of time. For people who are just beginning to practice, a small period of 15 minutes is generally the best option. 15 minutes is large enough to produce a difference in your mind-set but short enough to be easy to fit into your routine and not feel too challenging.

Finally, it's important that your meditation practice is consistent. Regardless of how long you chose to meditate for, meditating every day is important – just like it's important to maintain a good diet or exercise regularly, the benefits of meditation will only manifest if you meditate regularly. In general, it's best to meditate early in the morning when your mind is fresh and free from the thoughts and feelings that have built up during the day.

Chapter 12: The Lagom Parenting Style

It is even possible that we can take some of the ideas that come with Lagom and apply them to your experience and your work as a parent. Parenting is hard; there are so many opinions and parenting styles that it is hard to know what is the best one for your needs. In addition, it always seems like one person thinks that their style of parenting is better than what someone else will have. How do we know when we are parenting properly, and how can we add the ideas of Lagom into the parenting?

Although it is true that parenting is a matter that is very personal, and it will vary based on the family dynamics and the children in the family. Many parents will decide that it is worth their time to incorporate the Lagom beliefs and elements into some of what they are doing when they raise their own children.

Something that may not be that surprising here is that many of these ideas will come from the way that families in this country raise their children. Similarly, they may be based on concepts that are becoming popularized throughout the rest of the world. If you would like to learn more about how Lagom can be used in the realm of parenting, and you want to figure out how you can add this into your own home, and into some of the things that you are doing with parenting, there are a few suggestions that you can follow.

Let us start with something simple. You want to make sure that your child is getting enough natural light and natural air as well. This is important no matter what stage you child is in at the time - even as a baby. Whether this means getting them outside to play and enjoy what nature has to offer, or if it means opening up the windows and letting the air in while they play inside and take a nap, then this is what you need to do.

In Sweden, most of the doctors there will recommend all of this natural air and light to encourage the child to develop a healthy immune system and to feel happier. if your baby is dealing with some health risks that opening up the windows while napping could aggravate, then you can avoid this suggestion and go with something else in our list of parenting choices. This is also something that you can discuss with your doctor to figure out if it is right for you and your child.

The next thing that you can add into your parenting style when you are working with the Lagom parenting style is that you should spend as much time as you can with your children while also maintaining some balance. Families who live in Sweden make a practice of spending time together often, and they will even be happy to take a long and extended vacation together without it seeming off or out of the ordinary. Parents in Sweden will spend a lot of time playing outside with their children and will have a good deal of interest in what is going on in the lives of their children.

This may be quite a bit different than what we will see when it comes to an American family. Most of these families will spend a lot of time apart because the parents are working. The parents will sometimes go out with the kids, but often the kids are on their own and more independent. This is something that would not be seen when it comes to the Lagom lifestyle and the Lagom type of parenting.

On the other hand, it is also important for us to keep things as balanced and as in check as possible, and we have to remember that while spending time with our children is important, they are individuals. Children should have their own private time away from their parents and other family members on occasion too. It is important to spend time with them, but respect the boundaries that your children have, depending on their age.

Remember that, in Lagom, it is acceptable to work with childcare if it is needed. In Sweden, it is common for the parents to send their children to a childcare facility from an early age, and it is not something that is frowned upon when you need to get back to work after having a baby. Daycares in Sweden exist in many variations, and there are a lot of options out there for a family to choose from based on what is the best for them.

One thing to remember, though, is that while the daycare is just fine if it is something that works the best for your child, you still need to set aside some time after work and after daycare to spend some one-on-one time as a family with your child each day. This helps to keep that bond strong and will make sure that all of the emotional needs of your child are being met, even when you spend the day at work.

For a true lifestyle that is considered Lagom, children need to have some encouragement to play outside regularly. Parents also need to make sure that they are getting as involved in this as possible and should either be active with their children when the child is outside, or the parent should remain close by while the children are outside playing.

There are several reasons for this suggestion. It can ensure that the child is safe while they are playing and that if something goes wrong, there is someone nearby who will be able to help them out and comfort them. If something goes awry, the parent can fix the issue. Plus, spending time together, especially in the outdoors as much as possible, will help the whole family on many levels, including on an emotional level.

When you play outside, get more active, and have a lot of access - or at least as much as possible - to play in the fresh air and in the sunshine, this is a very important part of working with the Lagom lifestyle. In Sweden, it is not uncommon for families and their children to play outside, no matter what the weather is doing; families make a point to play whether it is snowing, raining, cold, warm, and everything in between.

As you can see, working with the ideas of Lagom parenting are a bit different than what you may be used to when you work with other forms of parenting. It is not helicopter parenting because it recognizes that the child needs to have some independence and has to be allowed to do things on their own, without a parent on top of them all the time. That being said, it also gives another opportunity for the parent and child to bond, helping to create a close family unit. It is important and it is only going to grow stronger when the family can spend some time together and work to reach a common goal.

No matter whether you spend time at work, or you get to stay home with your child, it is important that you spend some time as a family unit each day. Go to the park and spend some time playing. Do art projects or some other craft together for some time. Go on longer vacations together and sit back and enjoy that time that you get to spend together.

By the same token, it is also acceptable – and encouraged – to let your child go free some of the time. If your child wants to set a boundary or is looking to do something that requires them to be alone on occasion, then this is fine. You do not have to be connected at the hip to your child all the time. You just need to let them know that you are always there to love and support them and that you are their biggest fan. Recognizing that they will and do have their own lives - and they want to enjoy this as well - can ensure that they know they have that support, while still being able to grow and develop on their own.

This balance is something that is hard to do and stick with all of the time. But you will find that over time, and with some patience along the way, that this is easier to handle. You and your family have to spend some time figuring out what works best for you. Maybe you and your family like to spend more time together, and only a little bit of time as individuals doing your own things. Alternatively, maybe you like to spend more time doing individualistic things and then coming together at night to share and be a family. Always remember that the experience of Lagom is not the same for everyone who decides to use it. Some people will take a different path than what you may have considered for yourself. This does not mean that their method of using Lagom is any better or worse than yours. Adding in some of the Lagom parenting tricks and learning how you can live a happy and fulfilled life with your children can change the way that you view raising your children.

Chapter 13: The Lagom Lifestyle

We have mentioned several times in this book that the Lagom lifestyle emphasizes community spirit and collaboration. However, not everyone is fit for that kind of dynamic.

Some people are lone wolves. They do things better when they left to themselves. But that doesn't mean they can't work with others or contribute to any kind of group effort. The question is this—can the philosophy of Lagom work for them as well?

The answer is yes—they can apply this philosophy to their lives as well. Let's say you are more of an introvert and you prefer to do things on your own. Here are a few ways you can apply Lagom and create space for collaboration as well. The tips and ideas presented here can work both at home and at work.

ORGANIZE: CREATE A SYSTEM THAT ANYONE CAN EASILY PICK UP ON

Do you prefer that people do not disturb you when you're in the middle of something? That can happen to a lot of folks and not only to solo style workers and introverts. You can easily create or simply adopt one of the systems that the Swedes have used. For instance, to reduce office or home clutter you can set up a box, a basket, or even a box (any container that is big enough will do) at a conspicuous space. The Swedes put this bag or basket by the stairs so that everyone just passes by it and everyone can see it right away.

This container is where you will put every bit of clutter or misplaced item that is found lying around in the office. That way when something goes missing or when something is misplaced and have been found, it will just be placed in there.

And if anyone discovers that they may have something missing they can use that as some kind of lost and found section. However, here's the thing. When that receptacle gets full that is your signal that it is time to sort things out. Go through all of that stuff and put every item where it belongs. A small basket or a container that you can carry around will be better suited for that purpose. You can do that by yourself and if you have guests or visitors in the house you can quickly explain what that basket or box is for.

You can also apply this same principle in the office. You can put several trays on your desk or office. One tray is for requests that people want from you, another tray will be for notes that they think you should see, another tray is for stuff that other people wanted to get done that you have already finished.

You can also create this kind of organization using other items or other tools so that people can leave you alone to concentrate on your work. That way the flow you have going on while working won't be compromised. It's very hard to get back into full concentration after you have been interrupted.

SETTING UP THE AMBIENCE

Candles are a big thing in Sweden and it shouldn't come as a surprise that they are part of that Lagom lifestyle as well. In their culture, people would rather buy a lamp or some other form of lighting than buy some kind of furniture, like maybe a dining table or something.

Some people can dig that part about candles setting up the atmosphere and ambiance of a place while others can't. Some folks won't be too keen on setting up a lot of candles in the house like the Swedes do. That is especially true if there are kids in the house. You don't want to start a fire because your kid knocked down a candle by accident. But it's not exactly about the candles that make them such a huge thing in Sweden. What you're looking for is the effect of the lighting and the scent of the candles. The light effect and scent have a direct impact on a person's mood.

You can install dimmers in your house to adjust the lighting. You can set it to brighter light to keep you more alert and to help you concentrate on work. You can dim the lights to induce a more relaxed atmosphere when you need it.

You can use essential oils with electric diffusers and place them in strategic areas in the office or in your home. You can use this combination of lights and scents to improve the mood if the day turns out to be particularly stressful.

This is one practice that will be particularly useful during the cold winter months when the nights are longer. You won't get enough sunlight so you can do what you can and create artificial light to balance your mood. The scent of candles or from essential oils can help soothe your soul.

TV TIME WITH FRIENDS AND FAMILY

Now, here is something that American families used to have. It gradually disappeared with the advent of internet streaming video—thank you Netflix! Back in the day we used to have family TV nights where mom, dad, and the kids would gather around the TV to watch our favorite shows.

You can't do that anymore since we're all glued to each of our own screens. You can bring back this timeless tradition in your family at least once a week. You don't have to stick to the program on TV.

You can grab a movie from the internet too if you want. Choose something that everyone in the family can agree on. You can then prepare a family snack while you're watching it.

You can even rent a video if you want some old school vid that brings back a lot of fond memories. If you're living alone then you can invite a friend to come over. You can even catch up with a long-lost friend and invite them over for some popcorn and a classic video that you both enjoyed when you were kids.

It's not the show that is important. The important thing is that you can reconnect with friends and family and renew those bonds of friendship. Remember that it doesn't matter how much of a loner you are.

VEGAN OR SEMI-VEGAN DIET

Another part of Lagom philosophy is that of mindful eating. You don't buy food just for the sake of eating good food. Experts say that eating beef leaves a larger carbon footprint than driving a car.

That's how much the preparation and consumption of beef impact the environment. You don't have to be completely vegan 100%. You can be part vegan or just reduce your beef intake—that means fewer burgers or steaks a week if you know what I mean.

It will also mean that you should be taking more veggies during the week. Making that dietary change will improve your health. On top of that, you will also help the environment. Now this is a way to apply Lagom philosophy whether you're an introvert or not.

BARGAIN SHOPPING

The Swedes have lots of flea markets that they call "loppis." They love to buy second-hand items and they are usually sold for a fraction of the cost of brand new clothing. It's not just clothing that you can find in second-hand shops.

Sure you can find chic clothing too and they are sold very cheap. You can find a lot of items from lampshades to kitchen appliances. Just make sure to check the quality of the item before you pay for it.

There are also plenty of online stores that sell second-hand items. You can also practice Lagom by carefully and thoughtfully do some smart shopping for second-hand items. In a way you are preserving the environment and practicing Lagom as well.

This is again one way to practice this philosophy on your own. You can share this practice with friends and relatives turning it into a community experience if you want.

Chapter 14: Living a Frugal Life with Lagom

Finding the correct balance in life involves more than just your mental health – it is also about your finances and how you choose to spend your money. People who follow the Lagom lifestyle understand that it's okay to spend and splurge on occasion, but that clever frugality will provide you and your family with security and stability in your lives.

One way to achieve the correct balance is simply to be frugal in dozens of small, easy ways allowing you to save money for the more important events in your life. For example, if you are someone who buys your lunch at work, try preparing it in advance instead. A decent lunch can easily cost you $5 and this quickly adds up – that's $25 over five working days, $100 for a typical month and $1000 over the course of a year. That's the amount of money that could be used for something important; investments, car repairs, holidays, etc.

Fortunately, there are many, many ways to be frugal. To start with, try buying your staple foods in bulk and planning meals in advance, which is cheaper. Cooking meals in batches, then freezing or preserving these meals will be much more efficient than preparing meals individually and you can avoid spending money on snacks or fast food when you don't want to cook in the evening – just heat up a meal you have already made!

Perhaps more importantly, another way to save you money is to avoid paying interest whenever possible. Loans and delayed payments are almost always awful ideas as they end up costing significantly more than the actual price of the good. For expensive goods, such as cars, electric appliances or furniture delaying that payment of $1000 over several months, or even years, might seem immediately appealing.

However, why pay more for something than what it is worth? The interest on these types of payments will keep you cash-starved for months and years to come, which in turn can force you to rely on loans and delayed payments in the future. With wise spending, most payments with interest are completely unnecessary, so avoid these financial traps whenever you can.

On the same vein, if you have any debts your first priority should be to pay them off. Any money you save through frugality will be wasted if you are just leaking money through debts and interest already.

Another great piece of frugal Lagom advice is to understand when it's the correct choice to pay more for an item and when it's the right choice to look for a cheaper alternative. For certain items, paying for high quality will save you money, as better-quality items can last for longer and break less often.

Shoes are a popular example – cheaper shoes can be a ½ the cost of a more expensive pair, but soon the laces will start fraying, the sole will wear through and the interior lining will tear. In the end, you will need a replacement at least twice as fast, often costing you more in terms of cash and convenience.

As a general rule of thumb, for anything that can last for several years, or even decades, it's worth paying a little extra for better quality. This category includes items such as kitchen equipment and cutlery, workman's tools, any safety equipment and important pieces of clothing, such as suits, cocktail dresses or good-quality winter coats.

On the opposite end of the spectrum, it's often the right choice to look for the cheaper option when it comes to consumable items. This includes most foods and toiletries. Milk is milk, regardless of whether it costs $1 or $3; often you are just paying more for the 'brand' even when the product is exactly the same.

Likewise, items such as soap, shower gel, toothpaste can also be bought at a discount. It's true that there might be some nasty cheap brands, but you if you try a few different options you will find that in most circumstances, there's something just as good, if not better, than the brand you are used to for a fraction of the price.

it might seem harmless to spend an extra dollar on milk, but as touched on before, over the course of months or years it's these small expenditures that add up. You can buy more expensive milk, or you can save for a holiday or pension; the latter will undoubtedly have a bigger impact on your life!

Additionally, look to buy used items rather than brand new items whenever possible. Books, albums, electronics, furniture and clothes are all great candidates to get second-hand; if you look for bargains you can get items in good condition for a fraction of what it costs in retail. In most situations, people are selling these items to because they don't have room, or they need a little extra money themselves rather than the item being broken or damaged Many people already understand the various ways they may be able to save money. The difficulty comes, however at applying this knowledge. You might know it's in you best interest to save some money, but if you see that dres in the shop you might not be able to help yourself. Bad habits can be hard to eradicate and many of us find ourselves spending money on junk, even though we know better.

Fortunately, there are a variety of techniques you can use to keep yourself from spending too much. For a start, whenever you go shopping to a mall or supermarket, only bring a limited amount of cash with you; leave your credit card at home.

If you only bring enough money for what you intend to buy, then you physically cannot spend the money on extra stuff that you see around. it's still wise to have a small margin of error and bring just a little extra money, just in case something goes wrong. Nonetheless, by limiting yourself you can make it much harder to spend too much.

On a related note, always plan in advance what you want to buy. This means you can plan your route around a supermarket or shopping mall quicker, just navigating to the items you intend to purchase and reducing the temptation to peruse the other isles. Noting want that you intend to buy also helps you stay focused as you shop and makes it harder to justify impulse buys along the way.

Whenever you want to buy something that you don't immediately need (such as some tinned food or medicine) try waiting 1 month before making the purchase. If you are still thinking about the item after 1-month, you probably genuinely want it. If you forget the item (as you most likely will) it probably wasn't that important in the first place.

Above and beyond your capacity to remember things, waiting a little while before making a purchase is a good way to allow your emotions to settle. Even if you remember that you intended to make a purchase, chances are you might feel differently about the item if you wait a while. You'll probably realize that you didn't want it as much as you thought you did and that you are glad you didn't buy it straight away. Alternatively, you might also realize that there is a better choice of product that comes along.

Avoid keeping your credit card details saved on apps and websites. Platforms such as Amazon make it easy to buy anything with just a single click or tap; they remember your bank information and simply charge your account with the tab.

For people who know they spend too much, this makes life uncomfortably easy. With no barrier or effort in place to deter you from spending, it can be too tempting to say no. Avoiding platforms like Amazon might be the best option, but at the very least, you can change your account settings so that online marketplaces don't remember your credit card details – this forces you to go to the effort of entering them every time you want to make a purchase, which can help to limit your impulse buys.

It can also help to go shopping with someone who has a better handle on their spending habits. If you know you spend too much, try taking a spouse or friend with you when you shop, as their presence or judgment might help keep you in check. on the opposite end of the spectrum, if your friends or family members are bad influences, ensure that you shop alone and don't let them encourage you or spend time shopping that you don't need – there are many other things you can do!

It is possible for Lagom - when it is used in a proper manner - to even help you to save some money. This may seem a bit strange and may sound like a wild claim. However, when you learn how to live with just enough, rather than with too much and lots of excesses, it will result in you being able to make do with less, and that alone will save you money.

The idea of Lagom is not to go through your home and throw away everything until you have one pair of clothes and a few dishes to work with. The idea is to just learn how to have a nice balance with things. You can purchase things - but purchase them because they bring you happiness and contentment, rather than because you feel jealous that someone else has them or an advertisement convinced you There are several ways that the process of Lagom can help you save money, and they are pretty simple. just by following some of the other tips that we have already spent some time on in this guidebook, you will be able to work with Lagom in a manner that helps you to save money Some of the other methods that you can implement into your day-to-day life that will ensure that Lagom is being used properly and can help you to save some money include:

PURCHASE FEWER THINGS

With Lagom, you will learn how to purchase fewer things. You do not have to give up on everything that you want to purchase, and you do not have to live your life like a hermit to embrace the ideals of Lagom. That said, it does require you to learn how to just live with what you need, rather than having a ton of stuff that does

EAT LESS

When you decide to live the Lagom lifestyle, you learn to eat just enough, rather than too much. This alone will save you money because it helps you to learn how to cut out the excess of food that you consume and focus more on just eating what you want. Think of how small your grocery bill will go when you can implement this into your own life.

Plus, with Lagom, you are less likely to eat out as often, though you can still do this on occasion. However, your goal is more being responsible with your money and doing things in *just enough* fashion. Therefore, the eating out regularly, or all of the time like many Americans, would be out of balance; you need to stop doing this altogether. This could save you quite a bit of money all on its own, especially if you and your family spent a lot of time eating out during the week.

LEARN TO SPEND ONLY ON WHAT IS IMPORTANT

One of the best things that you will learn when you start implementing Lagom into your life is to spend your time and money on ONLY the things that are important. Lagom is a bit different than minimalism, as Lagom ideals are not about focusing on getting rid of everything; Lagom's focus is living with less. You will certainly try to downsize when you are going through this kind of process, and you learn how to not purchase as much in the future, but the focus is not going down to the bare minimum. It is more about finding a balance between purchasing just to fill a void and purchasing things that will make you happy.

LEARN HOW TO PAY YOUR DEBTS

While we are in this process of embracing the Lagom way of life, it is often recommended that you learn how to cut down on some of the debts that you have. The American lifestyle and idea that we need to buy more to be happier has certainly put a big dent in our credit, causing us to take on thousands of dollars in debt. This is often seen as the way of life at this time; we are supposed to have debt. We feel that we cannot get a car, a home, a college education, or pay for Christmas without having a credit card and lots of debt to handle it.

LEARN HOW TO IGNORE COMMERCIALISM

Ignoring the commercialism out there is one of the most important - although one of the most difficult - things that you have to do when it comes to implementing Lagom into your life and making sure that you can use this idea to help save some money. This commercialism is all around us. We see commercials and other advertisements saying that we need to get this product or another product to feel happy. We see our neighbors and family members purchasing something that may make us feel a bit jealous. We may even see things on social media, like people getting new homes, going on vacation, and more and we feel jealous – leading us to believe that we need to be doing some of the same things as well.

LEARN DIFFERENCE BETWEEN A "WANT" AND A "NEED"

Another thing that you can learn more about when you decide to implement the Lagom lifestyle is the idea of a want and a need. These are two different ideas; a need is something like the food you eat and the home you live in. A "want" is everything else, such as the special clothes you want to have, the books, the expensive car, and more.

Lagom is not asking you to get rid of everything that you own and never purchase a single thing. However, it can help you to save money because it allows you to learn what you need, rather than having you just go out and purchase things because you see it in a commercial, or because a friend has that item, or for some other reason. This can help you so much!

First, it will save you money. The less that you go out and purchase the more money you will save. When you stop spending money on items that you don't even need, not only will it help you to save some money, but it will ensure that you will be able to decrease the amount of clutter in your home, giving you more peace and happiness in the process as well.

You can use Lagom to help you to save money, as long as you are willing to fight against some of the commercialism that surrounds us all. You can live a very happy and productive life if we just learn how to live with just enough rather than thinking we need all of the latest and greatest things all of the time. This is hard to do sometimes, especially in a society where more is seen as best. When you are practicing Lagom, you can let go of this trap, the trap of purchasing more items, then having to work hard to pay for those items that no longer bring you joy or happiness after a short amount of time, and then doing it all over again. When you use Lagom to help you regulate yourself and take in just enough to help you feel happier and more complete, you can save money while also improving your quality of life.

Chapter 15: Lagom While Traveling

Another topic that we will spend a little bit of time discussing when it comes to Lagom is the idea of how Lagom can work when it comes to traveling. Many people love to travel. Whether it is a quick visit to go and see a family member or a friend, or a vacation with the kids, or on your own to some place that is new and exciting. A vacation can be something that we can implement into the process of Lagom.

Planning a vacation is sometimes a mixed bag. We are excited about the journey and where we are going, but trying to plan all of the details, such as where you should stay, what to see, how to get there, what to eat, and more can be a big hassle sometimes. Planning all of this and coming up with a budget to cover it all - especially if you are taking yourself and the kids - can give you a headache and often makes you wonder if it is worth the trouble and the stress in the first place.

The good news is that you can do the traveling and create all of those great memories at the same time! Let's dive in and see some of the steps that you can take to make this happen while maintaining your Lagom lifestyle.

Taking a vacation from work can be a good thing because it helps to create more of a healthy work-to-life balance, and for many people, it turns into an extremely relaxing experience. On the other hand, as we discussed a bit before it can take a lot of planning and execution to make the vacation all work out, especially if it is to a location that you have not been to in the past. All of this comes together to be extremely stressful in the process.

Traveling, depending on the methods that you use, can be a strenuous time for not only you, but for the whole family. Remember, the whole point of this is to have some time together, to take a break, and even to bond with one another along the way. This is what every family wants when they decide to travel together and have some fun, but sometimes, the plans aren't always going to work the way that we think they should, and this can create a lot of anxiety, discontent, and - of course - anger in the process. The idea of Lagom, if it is used properly, can help to fix all of these problems and give you the family vacation that you are dreaming about.

Practicing Lagom throughout your travels, as well as the whole time that you are traveling, can help you to stay more focused, help you to relax, and ensures that you can keep some of the mindfulness in your life as well. When you can bring all of these different parts together at the same time, they help you to form some stronger and longer-lasting memories of the experience and the vacation as well. Some of the tips that you can use to help make your travels more fun and relaxing while adding in some Lagom to the experience are discussed below.

Make some plans to help you stay organized, but do not stress out if you are not able to stick to them exactly for one reason or another. Things will happen in life, and no matter how well you plan and try to keep on schedule things are not always going to turn out the way that you would like. If you do not add in some flexibility to the plans, then you will end up with grumpy kids, anxiety in you, lots of fighting, and so on, just because of a little shift in plans.

For example, be sure to plan ahead in terms of scheduling the transportation that you want to take to get to your destination, such as a train a bus or a plane. You should also take some time to plan ahead to figure out where you will stay the night, such as which hotel you will use when you do get to your destination.

However, even these things will change. The plane may take off late and you will not be able to get to your destination at the time you had planned. Alternatively, you may find that the hotel you wanted to be booked up too fast and you now need to make some changes to get to the right location and have a place to sleep. Stressing out about this because it goes against your plans is not a good idea and can start to taint some of the good memories that you are trying to make. No matter how hard you try, things are not always going to work the way you want, and you will have a much more enjoyable time if you can take a step back and relax, rather than feeling dark and disappointed because things did not work out.

Outside of some of the necessities that we talked about above, try to keep most of the schedule loose and flexible. You can go and do some things as you would like to but realize that you don't need to be there at a certain time; leave things open in case someone is tired and needs a break. It is also a good idea to allow some downtime in the day, just hanging by the pool or at the hotel room, so that you are not rushing around the whole time.

Now, there may be times when you want to leave the country to do some of your own exploring and to have more of an adventure when you travel. Before you go, maybe consider bonding with your whole family as you try to learn a few keywords and phrases that will work in that country and in their language. You can also try out new foods in the area and visit some of the important landmarks while you are there

Always make sure that you are practicing the right kind of balance, and make sure that everyone in the party is respectful when it comes to visiting with cultures that are outside your own. You may not fully understand why a culture would want to take part in one practice, or why they like a certain food or holiday, but you can still learn how to be respectful and learn about their culture, rather than causing problems.

If you plan to head out to a destination that is pretty hectic the whole time, such as a major theme park or a beach that is pretty busy, then you should also plan some time to take it easy and relax into your day. If you can, set aside time when everyone can get away from the hustle and bustle and take a nap as they wish, or even have them just sit down and read or listen to their favorite music rather than having all of that stimulation.

Yes, being at a theme park can be a lot of fun, and there are always a million things that you can do while you are there

However, these experiences can have so much stimulation that it puts you out of balance, and your energy levels will deplete so quickly - much faster than they will do at home. Having this break to recharge is a great way to balance yourself out again after all that noise, those sights, and everything else that is out in the amusement park. Taking small breaks can help you to feel better and ready to take on more during the day.

It is also possible to take a vacation that is meant to just be relaxing and nothing else. You may assume that to go on a vacation you need to be out there, planning a ton of activities and running around the whole time to get the good memories. However, this is just not the case. It will end up causing you a lot of stress and headaches, and while it is sometimes fun to have a good plan, other times it is nice to just take a vacation, sit back, and relax during it.

Never underestimate the idea that it can be vital and so mportant for you to just spend some time together om a 1ew location, with some different scenery, rather than 1aving to be home all the time. Even planning a big racation can cause a lot of stress! Consider renting a big cabin in the woods together and hanging out with your extended family. Alternatively, maybe hit the beach and just have fun with the water and the sand and something good to eat and drink along the way.

These are just a few examples of what you can do when dealing with a true Lagom experience when you go on a vacation. There are too many families who are trying to make things perfect and planning every part of the whole vacation. While this may be done with good intentions along the way, it is not going to encourage the fun and the bonding that these trips are supposed to have, simply because it causes too much stress and too much anxiety on the whole family. Let go a bit, just be flexible, and realize that the most important thing to do here is to just spend time with your family and have some fun. If you can do this then you are well on your way to having a vacation that is balanced, fun, and going to help you to create some great memories.

Conclusion

The Lagom lifestyle can be difficult to achieve, but it's well worth the effort of trying. Seeking balance in all things can transform the lifestyle you already have, into a life that is fulfilling, rewarding, and vibrant.

Lagom doesn't claim that you need to quit your day job and travel around the world to find happiness and nor does it ask you to embrace a shallow spirituality. Instead, Lagom is found in the small things that make your life 'just right' - it's how you already live, just a little smoother, a little better, a little more Lagom.

If you are tired of your hectic lifestyle and you are looking for a way to reduce the stress, improve your mental and physical wellbeing, and ensure that you are getting the most out of your life, then Lagom may be the answer for you. In addition, this guidebook has spent some time looking at the various steps that you can take to get this done.

Whether it's doing your part for the planet, staying positive, owning fewer things or managing the turbulent world of relationships; hopefully, this guide can help you find that elusive and perfect middle ground - Lagom.

Decide how you would like to implement the ideas of Lagom that we have discussed in this guidebook. There are so many different ways that you can do this! Learning the right steps, and how to make them work for you, can take some time and some dedication. However, with a good plan in place - and possibly starting with one step at a time – you can make this happen and live a life that you deeply enjoy.

CPSIA information can be obtained
at www.ICGtesting.com
Printed in the USA
LVHW032058060521
686681LV00015B/898